Joong Suk Suh

The Glory
in the Gospel of John

Restoration of Forfeited Prestige

M. P. Publications
Oxford, OH

The Glory in the Gospel of John
Restoration of Forfeited Prestige

Published by
M. P. Publications
Oxford, OH

Library of Congress Cataloging-in-Publication Data

Suh, Joong Suk.
　　The glory in the Gospel of John : restoration of forfeited prestige / Joong Suk Suh.
　　　p.　cm.
　　Includes bibliographical references and index.
　　Appendix (p. 141-177) : Sociological theory for New Testament interpretation.
　　ISBN 0-932187-02-1 (pbk.)
　　1. Bible. N. T. John-Criticism, interpretation, etc.　2. Glory-Biblical teaching.　3. Bible. N. T.- Hermeneutics.　4. Sociology, Biblical.　I. Title.
　　BS2615.2.S84　1995
　　226.5'06-dc20　　　　　　　　　　　　　　　　95-10663
　　　　　　　　　　　　　　　　　　　　　　　　　　　　CIP

The Glory
in the Gospel of John

Restoration of Forfeited Prestige

Dr. Daniel Migliore

Joong S. Suh

To

Howard Clark Kee

I came from the Father and have come into the world; again, I am leaving the world and going back to the Father (John 16.28).

Father, glorify me in your own presence with the glory which I had with you before the world was made.... The glory which you have given me I have given to them (John 17.5,22).

In the world you have tribulation; but be courageous, I have overcome the world(John 16.33).

CONTENTS

Contents

FOREWORD

The analyses of the Gospel of John offered in this substantial work by a scholar who is currently a leading religious educator in Korea reflects the intellectual range, spiritual concerns, and analytical powers that he demonstrated when he was engaged in doctoral studies in Boston University. As his advisor, I urged him to pursue study and research not only in the more traditional fields of biblical history and exegesis, but also in classical studies and especially in the sociological field, to which Peter Berger had recently come as a pioneer in the sociology of knowledge. Joong Suk Suh evidenced skills and intellectual discipline in all these areas, together with the ability to integrate the insights gained thereby.

After his years of teaching and research at Yonsei University in Seoul, Korea, and extended periods of research there and in the U.S.A., the combined creative effects of his training and his unusual capabilities are now evident in this engaging study of the Gospel of John. He has read widely and understood well a vast range of theories and interpretive proposals about the origins and aims of the Fourth Gospel. But he has brought to each of these scholarly analyses his own rare gifts of insight, analysis and synthesis. These same intellectual gifts are evident in his critical study of sociological theory, and especially its bearing on historical and biblical interpretation.

Sociological approaches to biblical — and especially New Testament — studies are extremely common these days. In many such studies there has been an effort to adopt or adapt a general theory about social structures and products in simplistic ways. Examples of this are the use of structuralism, or the employment of generalizations about culture, such as group/grid theory, or the characterization of "Mediterranean culture" in terms of honor/shame. There has been little sensitivity to the diversity of situations in which Christianity emerged or to the complexity of the processes of its development in the various early forms of Judaism and Christianity as we now know them. What Joong Suk Suh has done is to maintain constant awareness of the interaction among social, cultural, and theological forces that is reflected in the diverse literature of early Christianity.

The effective results of this interdisciplinary approach are vividly evident in his analysis of the Gospel of John and of the specific segment of the early Christian movement in and for which it was produced. He faithfully surveys a vast range of secondary literature on this gospel, and demonstrates his own critical, analytical capacities. His approach is not limited to sociological forms or patterns, but draws on that kind of insight to illuminate and heighten understanding of the biblical texts.

Providing a fascinating, challenging — and potentially controversial — dimension of this study is the influence which he acknowledges as deriving from his own cultural context: "In the eastern religions [for which] the prime yearning... is to find unity with God in terms of reciprocity and oneness" (p.xv). With the current surge of interest in mystical participation among religious groups — including traditional Christians — there is an important message in this study of John, and the potential for development of a new and fruitful approach to biblical study and shared Christian understanding.

The extended essay which forms the Appendix of this book is "Sociological Theory for New Testament Interpretation." In an effective way, the author surveys major developments in broader sociological theory, and then proceeds to suggest the values and limitations of these different approaches for increasing

Foreword

one's understanding of the diversity and the processes of change that are represented in the New Testament and other early Christian literature. He is critical of both the macro-sociological approaches, which focus on larger groups or whole societies, and of the micro-sociological approaches, which focus on the role of the individual in his or her social surroundings. His own alternative, meso-sociological theory, seeks "to explore the possible links between subject and object, action and structure, and individual and society"(p.163). When this latter approach is employed for the anlaysis of the Gospel of John, there is a wide range of challenging new insights. The major emphasis is on the participation of the community of faith in the "glory" of the divine life. But there are also implications for historical understanding of some of the features of Gnosticism, for example. Some basic differences between John and Paul are highlighted, as well as differing estimates of the role of Peter. The extended bibliography will encourage the reader to pursue the issues raised so effectively in the book.

In the realms of method, exegetical analysis, historical reconstruction, and in such specific theological areas as christology and ecclesiology, *The Glory in the Gospel of John* makes a major contribution to the field of biblical studies. The interdisciplinary approach employed is both model and invitation for fresh investigation of these traditional documents.

Howard Clark Kee

Aurelio Professor of Biblical Studies, Emeritus, Boston University

PREFACE

This work was supported by Yonsei University Faculty Research Grant. The research focuses on the glory of Jesus and the glory of the Johannine community reflected in the Gospel of John. The glory is one of the most crucial ideas by which John's Gospel as a whole is to be interpreted. John's portrayal of Jesus' descent from heaven, his work on earth and his ascent to heaven can be illuminated in light of forfeiture of, struggle for, and restoration of the glory. The same scheme can be applied to the life of the Johannine community.

My interest in the Gospel of John was initiated by Raymond E. Brown and J. Louis Martyn who inspired me enormously in my study at Union Theological Seminary, New York. Further, my full-scale endeavors to John's Gospel were evoked by Howard C. Kee, Paul S. Minear, and Wayne A. Meeks, whose scrupulous interpretations of John stimulated and accelerated the present study. To these scholars I am greatly indebted for both challenge and stimulus.

The basic perspective of this work, however, is different from those scholars mentioned above, not because their theses are inept, but because this work has been prepared from the eastern religious proclivity in and by which I was fostered and influenced. In the eastern religions, the prime yearning of human beings is to find unity with God in terms of reciprocity and oneness. One of the major means to acquire such a unity is to presuppose their original status as gods and to work to restore it. In my study of John's Gospel, I have discovered that the similar idea can be found in the yearning of the Johannine community.

xv

I am grateful to the Committee of Yonsei University Faculty Research Grant which enabled me to explore the Gospel without financial difficulty. I wish to express my gratitude to the faculty members of Yonsei University who encouraged me to proceed with this research. I am especially grateful to Paul Stuehrenberg who appointed me as a Reserch Fellow at Yale University Divinity School and gave me full privileges in the library. My thanks also go to my graduate students for transferring the original manuscript into the computer and for proofreading it. As a token of my gratitude I dedicate this book to Howard C. Kee who was my mentor whose careful and creative scholarship provided a paradigm from which I invaluably benefited then and since.

Joong S. Suh
Yonsei University, Seoul
1995

INTRODUCTION

INTRODUCTION

The purpose of this research is to explore the characteristics of the glory of Jesus and the glory of the Johannine community reflected in the Gospel of John from a meso sociological perspective. The glory in John's Gospel, as W. Robert Cook articulates, is "not merely a motif *in* the Johannine corpus, but rather that it is the motif *of* the Johannine corpus."[1] It is remarkable, however, how little serious attention has been given to the theme of glory in John. Furthermore, neither the exploration in the glory of the Johannine community, nor the research on the glory of Jesus in relation to the community has been attempted.

One of the most substantial difficulties for interpreting John's Gospel is to determine the capacity of the evangelist. The problem lies in estimating the range of the role and autonomy of John. In form criticism John's role and autonomy are minimized, while in redaction criticism they are maximized. In sociological approach their levels are dependent on its subcategories. It is indispensable, above all, to determine John's position and weight not only in his writing of the Gospel but in his community before an exploration of a particular theme in the Gospel is initiated.

1. Relationship of John to the Johannine Community

There are three basic subcategories in the sociological approach: 1. macro approach, 2. micro approach, 3. meso approach. Macro approach is divided into two parts: structuralism and

---

1. W. Robert Cook, "The 'Glory' Motif in the Johannine Corpus," *JETS* 27(3, 1984): 291-297, quoted from 297.

functionalism. Both are similar in the sense that they emphasize on the fundamental patterns and processes of large-scale social relations. In other words, their focus is on the forest rather than the trees. Structuralist stresses on the social structure which constrains and determines the individual's thoughts and actions. Functionalist, who views a society as an integrated system of parts, attempts to explain some part of a system by demonstrating its unintended consequences for some other part of the system. These consequences are termed "function." In the macro approach, roles and autonomies of the individual are prominently minimized. The emphasis of the macro approach is on the constraining forces operating upon the individual's back. For instance, if we regard the author(s) of John's Gospel as the spokesperson(s) of the Johannine community, we are under the macro perspective.

Unlike the macro approach, the micro approach revolves around a face-to-face interaction among individuals. Micro approach focuses on the role and capacity of the individual within his or her "immediate" social surroundings. Micro theorists are interested in "choice" as the most basic aspect of human action. Micro approach is divided into two types: exchange behaviorism and symbolic interactionism. The former emphasizes on the common form of interaction, while the latter on the capacity of humans to create and use symbols as they interact. Both types concentrate not on the forest, but on the trees. In the micro approach, the ability and originality of the individual are maximized. If we regard the author(s) of the Gospel as the creative theologian(s), we are in the line of micro perspective.

Meso approach underlines a reconciliation between the micro approach and the macro approach. It explores the possible links between subject and object, action and structure, and individual and society. It concentrates on the relationship between the forest and the trees. Meso approach is divided

4

into two parts: structuration and interaction ritual chains. Meso approach, to form a link between micro and macro realms, is attempted by stressing more either on micro level than macro level, or on macro level than micro level. In meso perspective, the individual influences the society and is influenced by it. If we consider the author(s) of the Gospel as both the constructor(s) and the constructed of the community, we stand up in meso line. Indeed John is the creative theologian whose theology constrains his community, and at the same time he is the community spokesman whose statements are constrained by the community's proclivity. Wayne A. Meeks is one of a few exceptional scholars who disclose the correlation between theology and the community. He articulates, on this, quite definitely.

> I do not mean to say that the symbolic universe suggested by the Johannine literature is only the reflex of projection of the group's social situation. On the contrary, the Johannine dialogues suggest quite clearly that the order of development must have been dialectical: the christological claims of the Johannine Christians resulted in their becoming alienated, and finally expelled, from the synagogue; that alienation in turn is "explained" by a further development of the christological motifs(i.e., the fate of the community projected onto the story of Jesus); these developed christological motifs in turn drive the group into further isolation. It is a case of continual, harmonic reinforcement between social experience and ideology.[2]

Among the macro, micro, and meso approaches, the last one offers the greatest promise. In fact, meso approach takes a considerable step beyond the macro or micro way. The detailed explorations of these three approaches are beyond the scope of the present study. Theoretical grounds for these

---

2. Wayne A. Meeks, "The Man from Heaven in Johannine Sectarianism," *JBL* 91(1972): 44-72, quoted from 71.

three perspectives are presented in full detail in the appendix of this book. It is relevant to state that the presentation of this study has been performed from the meso sociological perspective.

2. The Johannine Community and Its Christological Strategy

The so-called standard hypotheses on the origins both of the Johannine community and its high-christology are to be reassessed. J. Louis Martyn detects in 1.35-51 the origin of the Johannine community which began among Jews who came to Jesus and found him to be the Messiah they expected. In the early period, they are called "Christian Jews" who live in a stream of relatively untroubled theological and social continuity within the synagogue.[3] The growth of this earlier group "aroused the suspicions of the Jewish authorities and led them to take severely repressive steps designed to terminate what they saw as a serious threat." The Jewish authorities began to persecute the group. This is a major feature of the middle period.

> Those who made an open confession were excommunicated and thus became a separated community of Jewish Christians who were then subjected to further persecution. The painful events of the Middle Period had lasting effects on the community's understanding both of Christ and of itself.[4]

In Martyn's reconstruction, some in the messianic group turned back to remain within the synagogue, while others were separated and alienated from the synagogue. The latter

---

3. J. Louis Martyn, *The Gospel of John in Christian History* (New York: Paulist Press, 1979), p.6.

4. *Ibid.*, p.7.

ceased to be "Christian Jews," and became instead "Jewish Christians."

> Expelled from the synagogue, the Johannine community was bound to search for a mature interpretation of the expulsion, and that search led it to new christological formulations. The logos hymn, for example, is probably to be assigned to this middle period... The *heilsgeschichtlich* pattern of thought presupposed in the earlier christological trajectory from traditional expectations to their fulfillment in Jesus is now being significantly altered by the dualistic, above / below pattern.[5]

Similarly, R. E. Brown, who begins to reconstruct the history of the Johannine community, proposes the existence of an originating group. According to him, the originating group of Jewish Christians including the disciples of John the Baptist regarded Jesus as the Davidic Messiah. It accepted the second group of Jewish Christians who understood Jesus as one who had been with God and seen Him. The acceptance of the second group "catalyzed" the development of a high, pre-existence christology, which led to debates with the Jews.[6]

The reconstructions of Martyn and Brown are creative and competent, but their presuppositions on the origins of the community and of its higher christology are less compelling. In Martyn, the standard Jewish "messianic group" does not become a unified group which originates the Johannine community, since only some of its members are excommunicated and establish the community. They did not possess a high christology in the early period before they were expelled. Similarly in Brown, the orginating group did not hold a high

---

5. *Ibid.*, p.105f.

6. R. E. Brown, *The Community of the Beloved Disciple* (New York: Paulist Press, 1979), pp.25–54.

christology. Rather, it comes from the second group. In both scholars, the originating group did not posit a high christology. Instead, they hold a lower christology.

Martyn and Brown presuppose that christology in John matches with the community's social experience, as Wayne A. Meeks has emphasized on a harmonic reinforcement between the two components.[7] The question of what sort of social experience does the high christology reflect, however, is not convincingly answered by them. For instance, the "expulsion" itself is not reflected in the high christology. Instead, it matches only with the rejection theme. Martyn articulates that

> socially, having been excommunicated and having subsequently experienced persecution to the death, they no longer find their origin and their intelligible point of departure in the synagogue and in its traditions. On the contrary, they, like their Christ, become people who are not "of the world" and who are for that reason hated by the world.[8]

It is obvious here that the "world" denotes the world of the Jews. After expulsion, according to Martyn, some of the originating group begin to define themselves as "Jewish Christians," instead of "Christian Jews." I suspect that the high, pre-existence christology itself does not reflect the social experience of expulsion. Rather, the pre-existence christology reflects the conviction of some believers that they have heavenly origin. After believing in Jesus the Logos, they began to reckon retrospectively that they had been in heaven before they were born on earth. What I undertake to argue is that, contrary to Martyn and Brown, the believers held not only the low christology but the high christology as well before the formation of the Johannine community. I submit

---

7. W. A. Meeks, "The Man from Heaven in Johannine Sectarianism," 71.

8. J. L. Martyn, *The Gospel of John in Christian History*, p.106f.

that some believers' high and low christologies with their acquired consciousness of their heavenly origin and their subsequent earthly limitation initiated the originating group which became a pre-stage group of the Johannine community. I suspect that the originating group, contrary to both scholars cited above, was a unified group which kept the high christology in addition to the low christology ever afterward.

The some believers' high christology and their own heavenly origin are closely interrelated, and cannot be easily separated. The same logic can be applied to their low christology and their earthly life of the flesh. The initiation of the community is dependent on these twofold christologies, and not on the expulsion from the synagogue. The believers are expelled, not only because they confessed Jesus as the Messiah, but because they regarded him as the Son of God / God, as the story of Jesus' dispute against the Jews in 10.31-39 implies. The expulsion, in opposition to Martyn, did not "originate" the high christology. Rather, it did "reinforce" the high christology to a certain degree. Furthermore, Martyn's reading of John emphasizes heavily on the one word, "*aposynagōgos*" (9.22; 12.42; 16.2) disregarding its equivalent terms to denote expulsion. Similarly, Brown stresses on this excommunication from the "synagogue."[9]

> Throughout the 80s there was an organized attempt to force the Christian Jews out of the synagogues. We see an echo of this in the *Shemoneh Esreh* or *Eighteen Benedictions* recited by the Jews as the chief prayer in the synagogues. The

---

9. Brown indicates that "it is impossible from the adjective *aposynagōgos* to be certain that John is not referring to one local synagogue. But the whole context of the introduction into synagogue prayer of the curse against the Jewish Christians... plus John's sweeping condemnations of 'the Jews'... makes us think that he is referring to the Synagogue in general." R. E. Brown, *The Gospel According to John*(i-xii), vol. I (New York: Doubleday & Company, Inc., 1966), p.690f.

reformulation of these benedictions took place after 70; and the twelfth benediction, ca. 85, was a curse on the minim or heretics, primarily Jewish-Christian.[10]

Although Brown does not confine his interpretation to this incident, alike Martyn, he rests heavily on the importance of this excommunication. Assessing Martyn's thesis that some Johannine Christians had been executed by the authorities of the local synagogues, Brown postulates another possibility.

> Nevertheless, I wonder if the situation may not have been more complex, especially since the putting to death is connected in John 16:2 with the expulsion from the synagogues.... once the synagogues expelled them and it was made clear that they were no longer Jews, their failure to adhere to pagan customs and to participate in emperor worship created legal problems.... Indirect participation in executions through expulsion from synagogues may have been part of the background for John's charges against "the Jews."[11]

Although Brown's range of interpretation is broader than Martyn's,[12] both scholars proposed that the occasion for the writing of the Gospel was the community's experience of expulsion from their synagogue, and that the Johannine community had been part of a Jewish synagogue before it was expelled. Thus, they emphasize on the Benedictions.[13]

---

10. R. E. Brown, *John*, I , p. Lxxiv.

11. R. E. Brown, *The Community of the Beloved Disciple*, p.42f.

12. On the recent revisiting to Brown see Michael Cleary, "Raymond E. Brown's View of the Johannine Controversy: Its Relevance for Christology Today," *IrTQ* 58(4, 1992): 292-304.

13. Recently, Robert Kysar endorses Martyn's and Brown's thesis that the Gospel was produced in response to the excommunication of the Johannine community from the synagogue. R. Kysar, "John's Anti-Jewish Polemic," *Bib Rev* 9 (1, 1993): 26-27, esp. 27. Kysar notes that "the reality is that an occasional writing has become canonical literature. Herein lies a dreadful danger!... It is to advocate that canonical authority resides only within an interpretative context."

But the Benediction does not contain specific reference to excommunication. J. A. T. Robinson's indication, on this, seems to be defensible.

> Unless one *begins* with a late date for the gospel, there is no more reason for reading the events of 85-90 into 9.22 than for seeing a reference to Bar-Cochba in 5.43, which has long since become a curiosity of criticism.[14]

Indeed the word describing the action in 9.34f., *ekballein* (to cast out) is so popular as to be used in "similar circumstances of Jesus himself (Luke 4.29), Stephen (Acts 7.58), Paul(Acts 13.50), and of Christians by other Christians (III John 10)."[15] The term *aposynagōgos* is associated with Matthew 25.32: "and he will separate (*aphorisei*) them one from another as a shepherd separates (*aphorizei*) the sheep from the goat." Martyn concentrates on the reference to exclusion from the synagogue 16.2a, disregarding v.2b which contains the reference to murder. I agree with Paul S. Minear when he finds that v.2b is a more significant index of date

---

Ibid., 27. Kysar's naming of the Gospel as "occasional writing" is not satisfactory. If it can be termed "occasional," all the rest of the New Testament, then, are also to be termed as "occasional." The Gospel of John has become canon, not because of its anti-Jewish polemic, but because of its high christology.

14. John A. T. Robinson, *Redating the New Testament* (Philadelphia: The Westminster Press, 1976), p.273. Robinson argues for A.D.40-65 dating of the Gospel. One of his grounds for this early dating is 5.2: "in Jerusalem there is a place with five colonnades." Robinson points out that John says here not 'was' but 'is' (*estin*). *Ibid.*, p.278. Wallace also argues for the pre-A.D.70 dating of John's Gospel on this verse 5.2. He demonstrates that the position which regards 5.2 as the historical present is less convincing. Daniel B. Wallace, "John 5, 2 and the Date of the Fourth Gospel," *Biblica* 71(2, 1990): 177-205, esp. 197-205. On the after-A.D.70 dating see Brown, *John*, I, pp. LXXX-LXXXVI.

15. J. A. T. Robinson, *Ibid.*, p.273.

than v.2a. According to him,

> in the first decades of the church Jewish authorities were
> directly responsible for assassinating their opponents as false
> prophets and teachers (Jesus, Stephen, Peter, James, Paul are
> only the known cases).... local decisions to exclude believers
> from synagogues were quickly and spontaneously taken,
> without waiting for formal authorization from any central
> rabbinic body... it is hard for me to visualize a form of
> exclusion more drastic than crucifixion or stoning.[16]

Minear's argument appears to be valid. Indeed the expulsion
from the synagogues, contrary to Martyn, occurred even
before A.D.80. However, it would be rash to affirm Minear's
conclusion that "texts like 16:1-3 are better mirrors of the
situaton in Judea before A.D.66 than of a more generalized
situation in Galilee or Syria after A.D.80."[17] The
presupposition that a text reflects a situation is not free from
difficulties. John writes the story of Jesus retrospectively from
his own situation several decades later after Jesus' death. A
text, thus, can often reflect various situations than only one
situation. At any rate, the expulsion from the synagogue is
not the most pivotal incident from which all the other
incidents in John are to be interpreted. The expulsion is only
a background of the Johannine community.

The community's initial experience of various rejections,
which include the exclusion from the synagogue, reinforces
and accelerates its high christology. However, it does not
necessarily mean that the community gives up the low
christology. Rather, the community retains it in order to
legitimate its own situation. The community begins to, and
continues to accept the other groups and their low or high

---

16. P. S. Minear, *John. The Martyr's Gospel*(New York: The
Pilgrim Press, 1984), p.55.

17. *Ibid.*, p.55.

christology. The Gospel of John, as James H. Charlesworth notes, "took shape over more than a decade."[18] Thus, the Gospel may be "the product of a group of authors."[19] It reflects the ongoing enlargement of the community.

The community has a twofold christological strategy. One is the initial strategy to propagate the low christology in public, the other is the main strategy to circulate the high christology in secret or in public, according to the social contexts. For instance, 1.35-51 reflects the former, while the substances of the prologue (1.1-18) and the farewell discourses(13.31-17.26) reveal the latter. 9.22 represents the community's initial strategy of the low christology.

These twofold christologies are altogether important for the community. The low christology, which presupposes the flesh of Jesus, legitimates the community's earthly life with limitation of the flesh, while the high christology, which retrospects and prospects the glory of Jesus' heavenly status, reflects the community's consciousness of former and future glory in heaven. However, the experience of being rejected in various forms[20] accelerates the high christology.

By being rejected by the world the community members had experienced the trauma of social dislocation. Their task was one of seeking and establishing a new place for

---

18. James H. Charlesworth, "Reinterpreting John. How the Dead Sea Scrolls Have Revolutionized Our Understanding of the Gospel of John," *Bib Rev* 9(1, 1993): 19-25, 54, esp. 25.

19. *Ibid.*, 25. Finding the affinities between the Dead Sea Scrolls and John's Gospel, Charlesworth articulates that "the theme of John 15-17 is Jesus' appeal to God that his followers be *one*. The only document prior to John that stresses this theme, and even applies the term oneness(*yahad*) - or Community - to the Qumran sect, is the Rule of the Community. Perhaps Essenes, now converted to the belief in Jesus as the Christ and living in the Johannine school, caused the inclusion of the chapters in the final edition of John." *Ibid.*, 25.

20. The most extreme form is not the expulsion, but the attempt to kill the communty members(16.2; 11.53).

themselves. How did they achieve this task? Jesus'
conversation with the Samaritan woman reflects their method:

> But the hour is coming, and now is, when the true worshipers
> will worship the Father in spirit and truth, for such the Father
> seeks to worship Him. God is spirit, and those who worship
> him must worship in spirit and truth(4.23-24).

John tries to reposit the place of his community in a new
entity and a new sphere, namely in the spirit. The spirit is an
invisible reality which is in opposition to the visible place.
After being rejected by the world they began to counterreject
the visible place, and began to reposit themselves in the
invisible sphere. This is a reason why the Johannine Jesus
presents the statement emphatically: "the hour is coming
when neither on this mountain nor in Jerusalem will you
worship the Father"(4.21). Now the community's new place
and new identity have been established.

3. Concept of Glory

The terms "glory"(*doxa*) and "glorify"(*doxazō*) occur 42
times in John's Gospel. These occurrences are remarkable
when they are compared to those of the other Gospels. For
instance, the terms appear only 4 times in Mark's Gospel and
12 times in Matthew's Gospel. Walter Bauer presents four
major divisions in the semantic range of the noun "*doxa*" : 1.
"brightness" or "radiance," 2. "magnificence," 3. "fame" or
"honor," and 4. an "office." He also lists two major divisions
in the semantic range of the verb "*doxazō*": 1. "honor" or
"magnify," 2. "to clothe in splendor."[21] Among Bauer's
general four categories in regard to the noun "glory", the
second or third is outstanding in the Gospel of John. Although

---

21. *A Greek-English Lexicon of the New Testament and Other
Early Christian Literature*, 1979 ed., s.v."Doxa," by W. Bauer.

some of John's usage of "*doxa*" insinuate "radiance" of the first division(e.g.,1.14; 2.11), they are also to be interpreted from the perspective of the second or third division. The verb "*doxazō*," which is derived from *doxa*, shares in full its peculiar linguistic history. It presupposes the usage of the noun *doxa*. John's usage of the verb belongs to "honor" or "magnify" in the first division of the verb.

Doxa in the LXX is the translation of *kābôd* which refers to the impressiveness or magnificence of God or of great humans. When used of God it describes the divine nature in terms of His power, honor, and self-manifestation. Gehard Kittel observes that in the LXX the primary meaning of *doxa* "does not emerge except with reference to God."[22] There is a tension between those who regard the LXX as retaining distinctly Biblical thought and those who make little distinction between LXX and *Koine* Greek. The assessment of this tension requires another book, and is beyond the scope of the present study.[23] But some notes on the investigation of Carey C. Newman may be relevant here.

> A resignification took place through the process of translation; in terms of tradition-history, the LXX translators, by their linguistic choices, preserved the Glory tradition. Because *doxa* began to cover other divine presence terminology in the Hebrew Bible, the translators reinforced and added to the various strands of the Glory tradition- i.e., Sinai, theophanic, Royal, and prophetic.

The usage of *doxa* in the New Testament comes from the LXX rather than from *Koine* Greek. G. Kittel posits that

---

22. *Theological Dictionary of the New Testament*, II, 1967 ed., s.v. "*doxa*," by G. Kittel.

23. For the excellent recent study on this assessment, see Carey C. Newman, *Paul's Glory - Christology: Tradition and Rhetoric* (Leiden: E. J. Brill, 1992), esp. Ch.7.

in the New Testament, as in the LXX, the meanings 'divine honor,' 'divine splendour,' 'divine power' and 'visible divine radiance' are fluid, and can only be distinguished artificially. In content, however, there is always expressed the *divine mode of being.*[24]

Although this is the primary New Testament sense of *doxa* which appears some 227 times in it, this sense is not a strait jacket into which all usage of the term in John's Gospel can be made to fit. In the case of the Gospel the divine power or honor as a "divine mode of being" is prominent for the meaning of *doxa.* W. Rovert Cook underlines that

in the Johannine literature, with but few exceptions it is used predominantly of the glory of God or the glory of Christ.[25]

His note is correct as far as the primary objects of glory are concerned, but he fails to explain why John uses the term in this fashion, and what sort of social situation this fashion reflects.

Margaret Pamment interprets the meaning of *doxa* in terms of "selfless generosity and love" rather than "power."[26]

In the Fourth Gospel, God's glory is manifested *in* the suffering and death of the Son of man on the cross. The forceful effecting of salvation through God's power, pictured in the O.T., is replaced in John by the effecting of God's salvation through the Son of man's voluntary self-surrender: the gift of God's Son.[27]

---

24. *TDNT*, II, s.v. "*doxa*," by G. Kittel. Italics mine.

25. W. Robert Cook, "The 'Glory' Motif in the Johannine Corpus," 292.

26. M. Pamment, "The Meaning of *Doxa* in the Fourth Gospel," *ZNW* 74(1973): 12–16, esp. 12.

27. *Ibid.*, 16.

Pamment seems to interpret *doxa* in the Fourth Gospel in the light of Pauline theology. Her interpretation, however, is indefensible. For, unlike the Pauline Jesus who "emptied himself, taking the form of servant... humbled himself and became obedient unto death, even death on a cross" (Phil. 2.7–8), the Johannine Jesus retained and manifested his glory in the fleshy life.

Unlike the other New Testament writers, John's usage of *doxa* is peculiar. He presents the term in apparently distinctive fashion. H. Hegermann explains its peculiarities as follows.

> In contrast to Paul the consistent view of the pre–existence of *doxa* is distinctive. Just as God's *doxa* is prior to all created existence, so also is the glory of the Son, who was always "with God"(John 17:5; cf.1:15). At death he returns to the *doxa* "with the Father"(17:5), but on earth he never departs from the *doxa* of the Father, for the Father is always "with him" (16:32; cf.5:17). In his revelation in the world the *glory* as of the only begotten from the Father(1:14) is characteristic of him. The Father gives him a share of his *doxa* in love (1:18; 3:35; 5:20; 17:24).[28]

Hegermann's explanation is quite satisfactory as far as the glory of "Jesus" is concerned. What has not yet been recognized by him is John's notion of the glory of "the Johannine community."

Although the theme of glory can be more clearly discerned in terms of its relationship to the words *doxa/doxazō*, neither an exhaustive study on the words themselves in John's Gospel, nor a comprehensive research into the lon~ history of the words before their appearances in the Gospel will be attempted here. Only a brief presentation of the concept of "glory" mentioned above may be relevant in this present

---

28. *Exegetical Dictionary of the New Testament*, ed. H. Balz and G. Schneider, vol. I, 1990 ed., s.v. "*doxa*" by H. Hegermann.

study which covers only the glory of Jesus and the glory of the Johannine community.

CHAPTER I

FORFEITURE OF GLORY

CHAPTER I
FORFEITURE OF GLORY

1. Jesus' Forfeiture of Glory

Jesus descended from heaven

Jesus is portrayed as "one who descended from heaven"(*ho ek tou ouranou katabas*) in John 3.13. What sort of meaning does the descent have? The descent implies that the Johannine Jesus forfeits his divine prestige. He loses his divine position within the sphere of the divine God. In the divine sphere Jesus is equal to God. He was "in the beginning with God"(1.2). Furthermore, he is the Word who was God(1.1). The Johannine Jesus, however, is sent by God: "God sent the Son into the world"(3.17); "there is truly One who sent me"(7.28). The very moment when he is sent by God in the level of the flesh, he loses his equality to God. He is subordinate to God.

> Nor is he who is sent greater than he who sent him(13.16).

The Johannine Jesus reacquires his glory, when he recovers his forfeited divine prestige. The complete recovery of Jesus' former divine status is achieved when he departs from earth for heaven.

Although in a broad sense the Johannine Jesus is regarded to have ascended to heaven occasionally in spiritual communion such as his farewell prayers to God during the last stage of his earthly life, in a strict sense he ascends to heaven once at a certain moment after his resurrection: "I am ascending to my Father and your Father, to my God and your God"(20.17). The primary purpose of Jesus' ascension into heaven is to restore what he had forfeited. In the early stage of his life the Johannine Jesus "was not yet glorified"(7.39), and he sought the glory of the Father who sent him(7.18). In other words, the Johannine Jesus is considered never to have ascended to heaven in the early stage of his earthly life.

One of the possible, but less convincing candidates for rejecting this argument is a peculiar exegesis on John 3.13. In the second half of v.13, Jesus declares one exception to the statement that "no one has ascended to heaven": "except he who descended from heaven, the Son of Man." Does the perfect tense 'has ascended' (*anabebēken*) imply that Jesus had already ascended to heaven before his conversation with Nicodemus? Delbert Burkett, who presented a scrupulous exegesis on 3.13, is a representative who gives "yes" to this question. According to him, "the Son of the Man has ascended to heaven on some occasion or occasions prior to his discussion with Nicodemus."[1]

Burkett's solution produces a difficult question: at what stage of Jesus' earthly life did this ascent occur? Nowhere recognizing John's allusion to Jesus' ascent in the early stage of his life, Burkett suggests that it occurred prior to Jesus' incarnation. A major motif in Burkett's work is an emphasis on Prov. 30.4 as a significant biblical ground for supporting this suggestion. According to Burkett, the question postured in Prov. 30.4, "Who has ascended to heaven and descended?" is answered by Jesus in John 3.13.[2]

> .... the question in Prov. 30.4 expects the answer 'no one except God.' No human being has ascended to heaven or descended from heaven, but God has either ascended to heaven or descended to earth on numerous occasions related in the Old Testament. For the expected answer 'no one except God,' Jesus substitutes 'no one except the Son of the Man.' In so

---

1. Delbert Burkett, *The Son of the Man in the Gospel of John* (Sheffield, England: Sheffield Academic Press, 1991), p.84.

2. *Ibid.*, p.85.

doing, he interprets the ascent/descent of God in Prov. 30.4 as his own ascent/descent. What is attributed to God in Prov. 30.4, Jesus attributes to himself as 'the Son of the Man' in Jn 3.13.[3]

Burkett concludes that Jesus designates himself 'he who descended' or 'he who has descended' not with reference to one particular descent, but to "all previous descents."[4]

> As the manifestation of God in the world, he has descended to earth and ascended back to heaven on numerous occasions prior to the incarnation. He has descended most recently in the incarnation.[5]

Despite his meticulous labor, Burkett's effort seems to be more ingenious than convincing. Burkett's suggestion may be persuasive as far as an exposition on Prov. 30.4 is concerned, since the expected answer to the question posed in the verse is 'no one except God.' This expected answer makes it postulate that God's numerous ascents/descents have occurred as Burkett suggests. The author of the fourth Gospel, however, is never the one who mechanically transposes the idea implied in Prov. 30.4 into the Gospel. In Burkett's exegesis, the role of the author of the fourth Gospel is nothing but the repeater of the idea of Prov. 30.4. However, John's primary concern is not the transposition, but the transformation of the idea in Prov.30.4. Unlike Burkett's imagination, John transforms God's numerous ascents/descents into Jesus' sole descent/ascent in terms of his incarnation in the flesh and his complete exaltation after the resurrection. Burkett fails to perceive the significant difference between God's descent and the Son's descent. God descends of His own accord, while the Son descends not of his own

---

3. *Ibid.*, p.85.
4. *Ibid.*, p.86.
5. *Ibid.*, p.87.

accord(7.28).

His suggestion is an attractive imagination. Although imagination is an indispensable intermediary especially for interpreting difficult passages in the Bible, it is to be discarded without hesitation if it cannot be supported by the biblical document concerned. There is no single concrete evidence in the Gospel of John to support Burkett's assertion that the Johannine Jesus had descended and ascended numerously "prior to" the incarnation. In Burkett's scheme, incarnation is to be regarded as one of Jesus' numerous descents. The Gospel of John, however, presents the opposite direction.

> For God so loved the world that he gave(*edōken*) his only Son... God sent(*apesteile*) the Son into the world(3.16-17).

Both words, "*edōken*" and "*apesteile*" are aorists which refer not to continuous action in the past, but to the simple past tense. If Burkett's imagination is tenable, those aorists should appear in different forms, namely, imperfects. Unlike Burkett, the point of 3.13, then, may be paraphrased as follows: No human being has yet ascended to heaven. The only one who descended from heaven in the flesh (incarnation), the Son of (the) Man "will ascend" to heaven at the time of his complete exaltation. This paraphrasing fits well into the continuation in v.14, which not only presupposes, but anticipates the exaltation.

The remaining problem in this paraphrasing is how the substitution of "will ascend" for "has ascended" can be explained. The problem is solved by the examination of the evangelist's literary characteristic, in which the time of Jesus and the time of the evangelist are not easily distinguished. It is the evangelist, not Jesus, who is speaking here in v.13, as in many other Johannine verses. The evangelist is simply retrospecting on Jesus' ascension. Raymond E. Brown

24

provides a solid postulation.

> ... in the course of post-resurrectional preaching the clause
> [v.13] came to be understood as a reference to the ascension.
> In the Johannine references to Jesus there is a strange
> timelessness or indifference to normal time sequence that
> must be reckoned with(iv 38).[6]

R. Schnackenburg shares Brown's postulation. He, too, thinks
that the perfect *"anabebēken"*(has ascended) is taken either as
the perfect in a general statement ("can ascend") or as an
anachronism due to the standpoint of the evangelist.
According to him, it cannot be a general statement, since the
aorist *"katabas"* makes the context historical. He concludes
that the anachronistical "explanation is correct for v.13."[7]

Burkett rejects this anachronistical approach, but the reason
he rejects it is less persuasive. Burkett argues that
anachronism

> requires the unlikely hypothesis that the Evangelist writes from
> Jesus' perspective in 3.1-12, abruptly shifts to his own
> perspective in 3.13, then reverts to Jesus' perspective in 3.14.[8]

Let us turn to the 3.1-15 in order to examine Burkett's
rejection. The scene changes from the conversation between
the two individuals, Jesus and Nicodemus, to the conversation
between the two groups, "we" and "you"(plural) in v.11.

> Truly, truly, I say to you [singular], we speak of what we
> know, and bear witness to what we have seen; but you

---

6. Raymond E. Brown, *The Gospel According to John*, vol. I,
p.132.

7. Rudolf Schnackenburg, *The Gospel According to St John*, vol. I
(New York: The Seabury Press, 1980), p.393.

8. Delbert Burkett, *The Son of the Man in the Gospel of John*,
p.82.

[plural] do not receive our testimony(v.11).

How can this shift be explained? Here "I" denotes Jesus, while "you"(singular) Nicodemus. Who are the "we" and "you"(plural)? Does "we" mean exclusively Jesus and his own associates? Does "you"(plural) mean Nicodemus and his own associates? Certainly not. Here "we" reflects inclusively the evangelist and his present associates, while "you"(plural) the counterpart of the evangelist and the present teachers of Israel. On this, Paul S. Minear's explanation is excellent and illuminating.

> In saying we, the narrator associates himself on the one hand with Jesus and the other hand with other leaders who have seen and who now join in giving their testimonies.... The paragraph that follows (3.16-21) can be read as a succinct summary of that joint testimony, because in many ways it fits more smoothly into the time frame of the narrator than into the earlier time frame of Jesus.... John often indicates that he has in mind the whole story of Jesus, viewed in retrospect from his own time of writing. This becomes John's own testimony to his contemporaries.[9]

Furthermore, this explanation, in which the distinction between the past and the present is somewhat blurred, is reinforced by the phenomenon that the evangelist employs various tenses (past, perfect, present) even in a same paragraph(e.g., 3.16-21). Recently Gail R. O'Day uncovered the same phenomenon in other sections like John 13-17. He notes that throughout the farewell discourse(Jn. 13-17)

> the temporal focus seems to shift constantly. At times Jesus speaks as if the crucifixion/resurrection/ascension were a past event(e.g., 16:33; 17:11), at times he speaks as if his departure from the world is imminent (e.g., 13:33; 14:3), and at still

---

9. Paul S. Minear, *John. The Martyr's Gospel*, pp.4-5.

other times he speaks as if he were in the process of departing at that very moment (e.g., 13:31; 16:15, 28; 17:13).[10]

In this sense Barkett's rejection is untenable. Burkett fails to recognize the evangelist's voice behind the Johannine Jesus' discourses. The shifts between past and present are not "abrupt" but "deliberate" at least for the evangelist. The Gospel of John is dominated by "this sort" of the anachronistical atmosphere.

Jesus' descent from heaven means his forfeiture of God's status and prestige. If Jesus himself descended on earth of his own accord, "sacrifice" is more proper term than "forfeiture." But Jesus has been sent by God according to His will; "I have not come of my own accord"(7.28).

Jesus of flesh

The Johannine Jesus is deprived of his divine prestige when he is sent by God "into the world"(3.17). The statement, "the Logos became flesh"(1.14) is to be also illuminated in terms of this deprivation of glory.

Thomas H. Tobin, S.J., who explores the trait of Hellenistic Jewish speculation in the Logos of the prologue of John, presupposes that "*logos* was an important concept in Hellenistic Judaism and had a long and complex history."[11] He proposes that in Philo's work

both the conceptual frame work and some of the vocabulary are remarkably similar to that found in John 1:12, 14.... In

---

10. Gail R. O'Day, "'I Have Overcome the World' (John 16:33) Narrative Time in John 13-17," *Semeia* 53 (1991): 153-166, esp. 159-162, quoted from 153.

11. Thomas H. Tobin, "The Prologue of John and Hellenistic Speculation," *CBQ* 52(2, 1990): 252-269, esp. 256.

both Philo and in John 1:12, 14 the context is anagogical in the sense that both Philo and John 1:12, 14 are describing the way in which human beings are guided toward God. In both Philo and John 1:12, 14 the logos is described as having a special relationship of filiation... with God who in both Philo and John 1:14 is described as "Father."... the terms used (prōtogonos in Philo, monogenēs in John 1:14;...) are not the same. But the similarities of both conceptual framework and vocabulary are nevertheless remarkable.... it is difficult to imagine that the two are not part of the same Hellenistic Jewish tradition of interpretation and speculation.[12]

What is not perceived here by Tobin is the considerable difference between Philo's logos and John's Logos in the sense that John's Logos becomes flesh, while Philo's logos does not. Despite many traits of similarity between the two, this difference blocks off the hasty conclusion on the relationship between the two.

In addition to Tobin, the background of the Logos in John's prologue is explored by some scholars like John Ashton, Craig A. Evans, and Howard C. Kee. John Ashton, who seeks to find the Jewish wisdom tradition in the background of the Logos in the prologue, maintains that

there can be no satisfactory interpretation of the Prologue that fails to recognize the author's double interest: it is a meditation on wisdom offering a variation on a traditional theme; it is also a hymn to the Incarnate Word. And the juxtaposition or rather intermingling of these themes prepares the way for the climactic utterance of v.14. The writer's central insight is summed up here-the identification of Jesus Christ, revered and worshipped by Christians alone, with the figure of Wisdom.[13]

---

12. *Ibid.*, 261-262.
13 John Ashton, "The Transformation of Wisdom. A Study of

Ashton posits against the attempt to seek the Gnostic traits in the prologue.[14]   Contrary to Ashton, Evans chooses The *Trimorphic Protennoia*, a gnostic document, as the most promising   background of John's prologue.   He presupposes that the prologue draws from the similar "milieu which produced *Protennoia* (though not *Protennoia* itself),"[15] but he proceeds to further investigation.   Rejecting the dichotomy of either/or choice between the background of the Gnostic tradition and the background of Jewish Wisdom tradition in the Old Testament, Evans articulates that

> both *Protennoia* and the Prologue have   resignified the Wisdom motif of *sophia / logos* dwelling in   or among men.   For the Prologue this is expressed in terms of incarnational theology,   but for *Protennoia* this is expressed in terms of Gnostic cosmology.   Although both works have emerged from a common milieu the evidence for viewing one document as dependent upon the other is not compelling.   Rather, what we have is a shared trajectory or milieu wherein common ideas and expressions have been worked out independently.[16]

Another exploration on the background of the prologue has been attempted by Howard C. Kee. He presents the similarities not only between Isis of Egypt and the Logos of John's prologue but between Wisdom and the Logos.   In regard to the former, he investigates that

> in Egypt . . . as early as   the New Kingdom we can see that a more humane and personal role than those of Hu, Sia, or

---

the Prologue of John's Gospel," *NTS* 32 (1986): 161–186, quoted from 179.

14. *Ibid.*, 161, 185f.

15. Craig A. Evans, "On the Prologue of John and the Trimorphic Protennoia," *NTS* 27 (1981): 395–401, esp. 398.

16. *Ibid.*, 399.

Maat is assigned to Isis, who receives credit for acts of compassion, restoration, and protection.[17]

Among these scholars mentioned above it is Kee who recognizes the difference between the Logos and other figure(s) explicitly, although he stresses on the agreement among the Isis, the Wisdom, and the Logos who is described "not in some timeless, universal terms, but in the language and conceptuality of the Greco-Roman world."[18] Kee introduces one of the differences between Isis and the Logos: "the grace of Isis has its ultimate expression in law... but according to John the law, given through Moses, is now supplanted by grace and truth which has come into being through Jesus Christ(1:17)."[19] What should be explicitly disclosed in the studies on the prologue's background are John's significant modification and transformation of similar features in his writing.

The Logos becoming "flesh"(1.14) represents a human limitation. The life of Jesus in the flesh is never to be the same again as the life of the Father in the spirit. God is spirit(4.24). On this, George Johnston's insight is commendable.

> ... the incarnate Son, John must want us to appreciate, is not in exactly the same glorified state as he had been before the creation of the world.[20]

---

17. Howard C. Kee, "Myth and Miracle: Isis, Wisdom, and the Logos of John," in *Myth, Symbol and Reality*, ed. Alan M. Olson (Notre Dame & London: University of Notre Dame Press, 1980), pp.145-164, quoted from p.148.

18. *Ibid.*, p.161.

19. *Ibid.*, p.161.

20. George Johnston, "*Ecce Homo!* Irony in the Christology of the Fourth Evangelist," in *The Glory of Christ in the New Testament. Studies in Christology*, ed. L. D. Hurst and N. T. Wright (Oxford: Clarendon Press, 1987), p.127.

Recently, Werner H. Kelber, who interprets the prologue of John in terms of "centering and decentering," points out that

> apart from installing the *Logos,* the most important function of the prologue is to engineer his decentering from *archē.* What it announces as the "coming into the world". . . amounts to a surrender of his privileged position in the interest of human condition. The *Logos* was installed *en archē* only to be dislodged from it. In applying the incision at the most decisive point, namely at the origin, the prologue administers decentering, a deconstruction of its own ontological foundation.[21]

Despite his fresh interpretation, Kelber does not explain why John's prologue "adminsters decentering" in regard to the social context of the Johannine community which parallels it in a greater degree. However, his insight on the "surrender of his privileged position," may be relevant here.

The Logos-Son's pre-existent glory had been relinquished when he had been sent in the flesh. In the last stage of his life, he requests the Father to restore his former glory of the Logos: "Father, glorify me in your own presence with the glory which I had with you before the world was made"(17.5).

There are some scholars who object to this argument that the earthly Logos-Son had forfeited his equality to God. W. H. Cadman argues that the Johannine Jesus had retained it, and throughout his earthly life he has been in the bosom of the Father.[22] Ernst Käsemann shares Cadman's objection. Unlike Cadman's tendency, however, he regards John's christology of glory as the dangerous docetism. According to Käsemann's provocative argument, it is "present in a still

---

21. Werner H. Kelber, "The Birth of A Beginning: John 1:1-8," *Semeia* 52(1990): 121-144, quoted from 131.

22. W. H. Cadman, *The Open Heaven,* ed. G. B. Caird (Oxford: Clarendon Press, 1969), p.206.

naive, unreflected form and it has not yet been recognized by the Evangelist or his community."[23]

Jacob Jervell, who finds similar atmosphere in John, goes one step further.

> In the gospel of John it is amazing to see how Jesus' humanity has a tendency to disappear.... In portraying Jesus, the author of John shows us a Jesus who is more truly divine than he is truly human.... The author of John is not really concerned with the human aspects of the person of Jesus; his interest is in painting a picture of the divine Jesus.[24]

An eloquent spokesperson of this stance is also found in M. W. G. Stibbe. Introducing G. Theissen's portrayal of Jesus, Stibbe presents that

> Theissen's Jesus is an evasive Jesus, a Jesus with no definite contours, a Jesus who seems more like a shadow than a tangible human being. One of the attractive features of Theissen's novel is that this is a particularly Johannine presentation of Jesus... the author's characterization of Jesus depicts the latter as the *elusive Christ*.[25]

Stibbe argues that Jesus is characterized by his elusiveness. He also tries to explore the background of this elusiveness. What these scholars underestimate is the statement on the flesh in 1.14. Rudolf Bultmann also recalls a possibility of docetic reading of John's Gospel. The Revealer appears in human form as a shining, miraculous, and mysterious figure.

---

23. Ernst Käsemann, *The Testament of Jesus. A Study of the Gospel of John in the Light of Chapter 17* (Philadelphia: Fortress Press, 1968), p.26.

24. Jacob Jervell, *Jesus in the Gospel of John* (Minneapolis: Augsburg Publishing House, 1984), p.16f.

25. M. W. G. Stibbe, "The Elusive Christ: A New Reading of the Fourth Gospel," *JSNT* 44 (1991): 19–37, quoted from 20.

According to Bultmann, "His humanity must be no more than a disguise; it must be transparent. Men want to look away from the humanity, and see or sense the divinity, they want to penetrate the disguise — or they will expect the humanity to be no more than the visualisation or the 'form' of the divine."[26] However, Bultmann, unlike the other scholars cited above, demonstrates more clearly the other side of the Gospel.

> All such desires are cut short by the statement: the Word became flesh. It is in his sheer humanity that he is the Revealer. True, his own also see his *doxa* (v.14b); indeed if it were not to be seen, here would be no grounds for speaking of revelation. But this is the paradox which runs through the whole gospel: the *doxa* is not to be seen alongside the *sarx*, nor through the *sarx* as through a window; it is to be seen in the *sarx* and nowhere else.[27]

Despite his elaborate observation of the paradox in the Gospel, Bultmann fails to grasp that "the paradox" reflects the self-identity of the Johannine community.

The flesh itself lacks glory. The flesh in 1.14 is to be defined as one that forfeits the divine glory. Jesus had a mother (2.1-4; 19.25). Unlike Matthew and Luke, John for some reason never introduces the story of virgin birth into his Gospel. The Johannine Jesus experienced thirst (4.7). Sometimes "he was deeply moved in spirit and troubled" (11.33). He had argued frequently and logically against the Jews(passim). Even after his resurrection he was regarded to have flesh such as "hands" and "side"(20.27). All these portraits denote Jesus' humanity which is distinct from God's divinity.

Furthermore, the title "the son of Joseph" appears twice in

---

26. R. Bultmann, *The Gospel of John. A Commentary* (Philadelphia: The Westminster Press, 1971), p.63.

27. *Ibid.*, p.63.

the Gospel (1.45; 6.42). In first instance Philip designates Jesus as "the son of Joseph" as do the disbelieving Jews in the second instance. Is the title "the son of Joseph" mistakenly introduced? C. K. Barrett answers affirmatively. According to him, John "should allow Jesus to be ignorantly described as 'son of Joseph' while himself believing that Jesus had no human father."[28] Barrett argues that "The son of Joseph" is employed by the Jews to discredit the claim of Jesus' heavenly origin. In Barrett's argument, there is no room for the flesh in 1.14. The flesh here is to be considered merely as a disguised form of God. Another problem which Barrett's argument produced is on 1.45. Granted his view of the son of Joseph in 6.42 as a mistaken designation, it does not necessarily imply that the same designation by Philip in 1.45 is also mistaken. On this, C. H. Dodd explains distinctly. The words "Jesus of Nazareth, the son of Joseph" appear

> in a formal confession of Christ by Philip, one of the first disciples, and can hardly have been intended to be entirely erroneous. The intention appears to be to indentify Jesus as the son of Joseph from Nazareth, and then to designate Him as the Messiah of whom Moses and the prophets wrote, as Son of God, and as King of Israel; these titles being understood, not as contradicting Philip's description of his human identity, but as affirming that He who is, on the human plane, 'Jesus son of Joseph' is *also* that which these titles imply.[29]

Recently, Marianne Meye Thompson endorses Dodd's view. According to Thompson,

---

28. C. K. Barrett, *The Gospel According to St John. An Introduction with Commentary and Notes on the Greek Text*, 2nd ed. (London: SPCK, 1978), p.184.

29. C. H. Dodd, *The Interpretation of the Fourth Gospel* (Cambridge: Cambridge University Press, 1953), p.260, n.1.

Jesus' heavenly and earthly origins are mutually exclusive,
formulated as an either / or statement. But as Dodd views
the problem, the answer is not an either / or. That Jesus
is from heaven does not necessarily imply that he is not also
"the son of Joseph."[30]

The fourth Gospel tries to give an impression that Jesus, as
the son of Joseph, lives a truly human life in time and space
like his contemporaries. A description of G. Johnston may be
cited, since it makes the point admirably.

For this evangelist and his Church, the icon of the Father
must be framed unmistakably in divinity, and yet the face of
the icon is a Jewish face.[31]

Jesus has a true humanity (flesh) as these scholars
emphasize. The author of the Gospel, however, delineates that
Jesus, unlike his contemporaries, has divinity also. John's
Gospel starts from the axiom that Jesus is the son of Joseph
(humanity) and the Son of God/God (divinity). John has seen
both the divinity in Jesus' humanity and the humanity in his
divinity. John combines both transcendence and limitation in
Jesus. This axiom is important for defining the
characteristics of the glory in John's Gospel. What I wish to
argue is that Jesus who has both aspects of humanity and
divinity is subordinate to God who has divinity without
humanity (flesh). As a man is greater than a mermaid who is
greater than a fish, God is greater than Jesus who is greater
than those who have humanity only. Jesus' humanity is
more emphasized than his divinity in certain passages, while
his divinity is more stressed than his humanity in the other
passages.

---

30. M. M. Thompson, *The Humanity of Jesus in the Fourth
Gospel* (Philadelphia: Fortress Press, 1988), p.25.
31. George Johnston, "*Ecce Homo!* Irony in the Christology of the
Fourth Evangelist," p.129.

The flesh of Jesus means his forfeiture of God's status. Jesus' sense of forfeiture is deepened, whenever people admit only to his humanity, namely, "the son of Joseph." Many characters, including the disciples, in John's Gospel did not recognize the divinity contained in his flesh. The Johannine Jesus embodies transcendental divinity not only in his flesh but in his social surroundings, as the statement, "the light shines in the darkness"(v.5) implies. However, his contemporaries ignore his transcendental divinity manifested in his flesh and his surroundings. When people recognize his divinity in the flesh, the Johannine Jesus of the flesh begins the restoration of his former glory (12.23). The complete restoration of God's position is achieved when he rids himself of his humanity and ascends 'to heaven. Jesus remains unglorified in the flesh even shortly after his resurrection, since he has "not yet ascended to the Father"(20.17), and still has flesh such as "hands" and "sides" (21.27). The pre-existent glory of Jesus is regained, when his status moves from the inclusive level of both humanity and divinity to the exclusive level of divinity. The statement, "I go to the Father" (14.28) means this moving of Jesus' status toward God's divinity.

Jesus less great than God

The statement, "For the Father is greater than I" (14.28) is also to be illuminated in this context. Why is the Johannine Jesus, whose oneness with God is disclosed in various passages of John's Gospel, less great than God? George R. Beasley-Murray seeks the solution to this problem.

> ...the statement in v.28 is one with many representations in the Fourth Gospel as to the obedience of the Son to the Father (e.g., 4:34; 8:29) and his dependence on the Father for every aspect of his ministry(e.g., 5:19; 12:48-49).[32]

Beasley-Murray's solution is not untenable. But the question remains: why does Jesus obey and depend on God? The answer is that Jesus has been sent by God. The sender is greater than the one who is sent (13.16). In addition to this, Jesus has been sent in the level of the flesh which has no place in God (4.24). In this sense Jesus is subordinate to God. Barrett is convincing when he recognizes the different status between the sender and one sent. "The Father is *fons divinitatis* in which the being of the son has its source; The Father is God sending and commanding, the Son is God sent and obedient."[33] Despite his convincing point on the difference between the sender and one sent, Barrett fails to discern the real reason why God is greater than Jesus in regard to the difference between one who has the flesh and one who has not.

Jesus' divinity is to be disclosed in the flesh, yet the flesh itself is not constituted with divinity. The flesh itself is never regarded to be divine in John's Gospel. "That which is born of the flesh is flesh, and that which is born of the Spirit is spirit"(3.6). There are several aspects which show the subordination of the Johannine Jesus with the flesh to God. He does not speak on his own authority; but the Father who dwells in him does His works (14.10). The reason that Jesus is working is that his "Father is working still" (5.17). The purpose of Jesus' working is to do the will of Him who sent him, and to accomplish His work(4.34; cf. 9.4). In addition to this aspect, the Johannine Jesus does not seek his own glory, but the glory of Him who sent him (7.18). He prays "Father, glorify your name" (12.28). Even when he asks for the glory he does it for glorifying God: "glorify your Son that the Son may glorify you" (17.1).

The achievement of Jesus' recovery of his former divine

---

32. Gerge R. Beasley-Murray, *John.* Word Biblical Commentary 36 (Waco, Texas: Word Books, 1987), p.262.

33. C. K. Barrett, *The Gospel According to St John*, p.468.

glory is dependent exclusively on God's will and His permission. The Johannine Jesus prays to God for His permission on this recovery. "Father, glorify me in your own presence with the glory that I had with you" (17.5). In restoration of his former glory, Jesus' dependence on the Father's initiative is explicit and decisive in John. This is another dimension of the statement that God is greater than Jesus (14.28).

2. The Community's Forfeiture of Glory

Behind the characteristics of John's portrayal of Jesus who has been sent by God into the world, there is the Johannine community which influences John in a greater degree. The recognition of the existence of the Johannine community is indispensable for interpreting John. One of the most prominent works to coherently connect John's description of Jesus to the Johannine community is that of Wayne A. Meeks. With the publication of Meeks' significant article, "The Man from Heaven in Johannine Sectarianism,"[34] new perpective of the study on John has been announced. Meeks demonstrates in this article that

> the Fourth Gospel not only describes . . . the birth of that community; it also provides reinforcement of the community's isolation. The language patterns we have been describing have the effect, for the insider who accepts them, of demolishing the logic of the world, particularly the world of Judaism, and progressively emphasizing the sectarian consciousness. If one "believes" what is said in this book, he is quite literally taken out of the ordinary world of social

---

34. *JBL* 91 (1972): 44-72.

reality.[35]

Meeks' perspective here appears to be convincing. His work has greatly impacted the subsequent studies on John as seen from this perspective. Recently, Warren Carter tries to revise some of Meeks' arguments, but his revision is questionable. Quoting Meeks' statement "the community's social identity... appears to have been largely negative," Carter postulates as follows.

> Rejected and socially alienated, yes; but a negative identity, no. Only in this community is God's revelation, presence and wisdom to be disclosed.[36]

I suspect that Carter's revision is inappropriate. For Meeks, the term "negative" denotes community color not from its own perspective, but from the view of the larger society. Carter tries to argue that

> as the community has recognized and accepted the divine claim of Jesus, so society has rejected it. By this rejection, the community's belief is legitimated, and the opponents and rivals, and their claims, are shown to be illegitimate and invalid... On the basis of such divine reality, reflected in social events, the community is constituted.[37]

I do not find any major differences between Meeks and Carter at least in the argument cited above. Carter says nothing new, but rather offers a paraphrased repetition of Meeks' thesis in this regard. The community's social identity appears to be "negative"(Meeks) if we see it from the perspective of the

---

35. *Ibid.*, 71.

36. Warren Carter, "The Prologue and John's Gospel: Function, Symbol and the Definitive Word," *JSNT* 39 (1990): 35-58, quoted from 49f.

37. *Ibid.*, 50.

larger society. At the same time it appears to be "positive" (Carter) if we view it from the perspective of the insiders of the community, although the *forms* of the community's self-expression are "largely negative."

Paul S. Minear has produced a work on John from a similar perspective in terms of integrating Jesus in John to the Johannine community. In regard to the prologue of John, he points out that

> the most obvious trace of his work is an occasional use of the first person pronoun in the opening chapter, for instance: "And the Word... dwelt among us...; we have beheld his glory... [1:14]." Such a statement clearly implies that the entire opening confession should be read as "our" confession. The narrator is writing as a believer and as a member of a community of believers who have seen and bear witness to the glory of this Word, this Son. The choice of *we* rather than I suggests that the narrator is writing not only himself but also as a representative of a larger group, either the whole company of believers or a limited group of its leaders who have been granted a vision of the glory.[38]

In fact, the descriptions of Jesus in John and the situation of the Johannine community behind them are not to be easily separated, as Minear's postulation indicates. The story of Jesus in John is the story of the Johannine community.

Believers born of God

How does the members of the Johannine community define themselves? First of all, they recognize themselves as "gods."

If he called them gods to whom the word of God came... (10.35).

---

38. Paul S. Minear, *John. The Martyr's Gospel,* pp.3-4.

Although the designation "gods" appears in the context of
Jesus' controversy against the misunderstanding of the Jews
on his divine origin, it insinuates the self-definition of the
community. Its members perceive themselves as "gods." At
what stage of their life did this self-consciousness of "gods"
commence? It occurred after believing in Jesus who became
flesh and prior to formation of the community on this belief.
On one hand, they are "gods" to whom the word of God
came (10.35), as Jesus is the One to whom the words of God
have been given (17.8). On the other hand, they are "children
of God" (1.12) and "those born of God" (1.13), as Jesus, who
descended from heaven, is "Son of God" (3.18) and "came
from the Father" (16.27,28). The community members define
their community as "the divine community." This definition
is implicitly disclosed in the prologue of John.

Where is the pivot of the prologue? R. Alan Culpepper
presents a chiasm, with its seven stage progression balancing
vv.1-2 / v.18 , v.3 / v.17 , vv.4-5 / v.16 , vv.6-8 / v.15 ,
vv.9-10 / v.14 , v.11 / v.13 , and v.12a / v.12c. He finds its
pivot in v.12b.[39] Culpepper criticizes M. E. Boismard that
Boismard fails to separate v.11 from v.10. In Culpepper, "the
structure suggested here allows these verses to be separated."
The reason for this separation, according to him, is that "v.11
changes from 'world' to 'his own' and is balanced by
v.13."[40] However, Culpepper's criticism is less compelling.
Verse 10c and v.11 cannot be separated, since "world" in
v.10c and "his own" in v.11, contrary to Culpepper, are
introduced as similar subjects who respond negatively to the
Logos.

Furthermore, his attempt to parallel v.11 to v.13 is far from
obvious, since the term and content in v.11 and v.13 are not
easily balanced. One of the major terms he chooses, *"hoi*

---

39. R. Alan Culpepper, "The Pivot of John's Prologue," *NTS* 27
(1981): 1-31, esp. 16.
40. *Ibid.*, 17.

idioi auton" in v.11 does not appear in v.13. In regard to content, "those born of God" in v.13 is paralleled not to "his own" in 11, but to "the children of God" in v.12. Culpepper's endeavor to separate v.12 from v.13 is also confusing and probably confused, since v.13 is only to give additional explanation to v.12. His choice of "the children of God" as the most pivotal term is very satisfactory, but his construction of a chiasm in the prologue cannot be sustained. Culpepper proposes that

> the interpreter must also bear in mind that all literary structures are varying degrees artificial. The prologue of John is a work of art; the artist used structures, but he was not their slave. To have made the chiastic structure more explicit would necessarily have made it more artificial.[41]

Although this proposition is valid, cautions are called for the chiastic approaches whose proclivity easily captures the chiastic scholars under the net of chiasmania.

We will be on safer ground if we include all of vv.10c-13 in the pivot of the prologue.[42] The reason for this inclusion is that there is no exact parallel of vv.10c-13, in contrast with parallels of vv.1-10a to vv.14-18. John emphasizes on the contrast between those who rejected the Logos and those who

---

41. *Ibid.*, 17.

42. On the recent attempt to regard v.11 as the central section of the prologue, see John W. Pryor, "Jesus and Israel in the Fourth Gospel-John 1:11," *Nov Test* 32(3, 1990): 201-218. Pryor argues that "the reference in v.11 is exclusively to the mission of the incarnate Logos to Israel, his people *kata sarka*" (*Ibid.*, 201), and concludes that "Israel,... his own people by race, have shown by their rejection of him to belong totally to the world" (*Ibid.*, 218). Ed. L. Miller, who is in a different line, regards vv.1-5 as pivotal section which contains a complete Logos hymn. It became "the logical foundation-piece of the rest of the Prologue material." Ed. L. Miller, "The Logic of the Logos Hymn: A New View," *NTS* 29(1983): 552-561, quoted from 552.

accepted the Logos. The conflict between them is manifested throughout the Gospel. Thus, it is natural to posit the pivot of the prologue in verses 10c-11 which reflect and condense the same conflict.

The pivot of the prologue is verses 10c-13, where not only are the two different responses to Jesus who became flesh introduced in terms of the rejection by his own people and the reception by the believers who become the children of God, but the divine origin of the Johannine community is insinuated as well. That these pivotal verses have often not been included in Kelber's work is manifestly indefensible. In interpreting the prologue in terms of "centering and decentering," Kelber articulates that

> the centering and decentering operations of the prologue narrate three beginnings: the beginning of the *Logos* who is grounded in the preexistent archē (John 1:1), the beginning of John (the baptizer) whose witness introduces Jesus' ministry (John 1:6-8,15), and Jesus' own earthly beginning which sets the stage for his incarnational mission (John 1:14). John's threefold beginnings signify three stages of Jesus' *archē*: the transcendental origin, his historical inauguration, and his own incarnational commencement . . . The making of a beginning has a way of begetting more beginnings, and the more distanced the primary beginning, e.g. the origin, the greater the need for decentering and successive beginning.[43]

What characterizes this study is the absence of exploring the sociological implications behind the purpose for the making of a beginning with threefold "decentering and successive beginnings." The Johannine community, whose influence on John is strong, is minimized in Kelber's scheme. Consequently, the pivotal verses 10c-13 are underestimated by him. Furthermore, he forgets in the last part of his article

---

43. Werner H. Kelber, "The Birth of A Beginning: John 1:1-8," 131-132.

what he had argued before in the middle part of it. He had argued that the prologue has three beginnings as it is cited above. Later, he adds one more beginning to these three without any explanations for this alteration.

> Creation of authority which legitimates the *Logos* at various stages of beginning – transcendentally versus the *logoi*, anteriorly vis-á-vis John the Baptizer, incarnationally against "his own" but on behalf of the "children of God," and ontotheologically in opposition to Mosaic ascent mysticism – is thus a central feature of the johannine prologue.[44]

Kelber insinuates four beginnings here in contrast to three beginnings in earlier part. It would be more convincing than the present form if he had produced in earlier part four categories of beginning instead of three, inserting "the beginning of responses, which presuppose the beginning of the Johannine community, to the *Logos*."

Warren Carter categorizes the themes contained in the prologue into four parts: 1. the origin and destiny of the *Logos,* 2. Jesus' role as the revealer, 3. responses to Jesus, and 4. the relationship of Jesus to other figures.[45] In regard to 3, Carter divides them into two types of negative and positive responses. For the latter, he allocates the explanation on the phrase of "children of God" to only a few lines.[46] Carter argued in the earlier part of his article that "the Prologue is to be viewed as part of the Gospel's 'cluster of sacred symbols,' which legitimates and interprets the experiences and self-understanding of John's community."[47] But it is remarkable how little serious attention has been given by him to the exploration on the birth of the Johannine

---

44. *Ibid.*, 140.

45. Warren Carter, "The Prologue and John's Gospel: Function, Symbol and the Definitive Word," 37.

46. *Ibid.*, 39.

47. *Ibid.*, 35.

community which produced John's prologue.

Apart from a chiastic analysis, the other reason why the verses 10c-13 form the pivot of John's prologue is that the whole prologue is the product of John (whoever he is) whose primary reference group is the Johannine community. The prologue is retrospectively produced from the time of the evangelist. In this regard, the verses 10c-13 which contain the decisive self-definition of the community, are to be regarded as the pivotal part of the prologue.

One of the most prominent self-identity of the Johannine community is the "children of God" (*tekna theou*) and "those born of God" (*hoi... ek theou egennēthēsan*).[48] The relationship between the two designations is to be explained in the sense that the latter emphasizes more on the divine origin of the community members, while the former more on the present status as a result of being born of God. The Johannine community is the divine community in terms of its origin and its consciousness of its present state.

The phrase, "those born *of* (*ek tou*) *God* " means that the Johannine community members regard themselves as those who came *from* (*ek tou*) God, whose dwelling place is in heaven. As Jesus came from heaven, so they also came from heaven. It insinuates their original dwelling place was in heaven. Thus, as Jesus forfeits the divine glory when he came from heaven, the members of the community also forfeit the divine glory when they came from heaven. Carter underscores that

---

48. Except for some Latin texts and Latin testimonies from Origen and Augustine in which the singular instead of the plural "*hoi*" is present, most texts have the plural. Majority of modern scholars, like R. E. Brown, R. Schnackenburg, C. K. Barrett, prefer the plural. On the difficult problems of the singular reading, see, J. W. Pryor, "Of the Virgin Birth or the Birth of Christian? The Text of John 1:13 Once More," *Nov Test* 27(4, 1985): 296-318.

rather Jesus the *logos* is the revelation (10.30; 14.9). In replacing the ascent-descent pattern with a descent-ascent schema, the Prologue and Gospel radically shift the emphasis - a starting point of heaven not earth, a divine not angelic or human figure, earth not heaven as the visited sphere, a revealer who has intimately known and seen God, and in whom God is manifested.[49)]

Carter's argument is competent and compelling, as far as the statement on Jesus the Logos is concerned. However, he does not perceive that John's radical "shift" of "the emphasis" reflects the community members' experience of radical shift on self-definition of their identity. What I assert is that before they believed in Jesus the Logos, they understood themselves as those who came from earth, not heaven, but after believing in him, they begin to define themselves retrospectively as those who came from heaven, not earth. The community members begin to regard themselves as those whose origin was in heaven, but they came from God who is in heaven, and presently live on earth. Although they keep in mind their heavenly origin, their present earthly life is to be illuminated in terms of forfeiture of their heavenly prestige.

Believers of flesh

Although the members of the Johannine community retain the heavenly origin in their own consciousness, they are born of flesh and live with flesh on earth like their own contemporaries. They could not survive without flesh. Jesus of flesh "dwelt among" their fleshes(1.14). The flesh is indispensable for their life, as it is for Jesus' life. There have been some amounts of discussion on the statement, "who were born, not of blood nor of the will of the flesh nor

---

49. Warren Carter, "The Prologue and John's Gospel: Function, Symbol and the Definitive Word," 45.

of the will of man, but of God"(1.13). The heavy exploration on the phrase, "nor of the will of the flesh," however, has not yet been attempted.

The "will of the flesh" may denote "sexual desire," as George R. Beasley-Murray suggests.[50]   However, it is introduced not to degrade the desire, but to enunciate the supernatural origin of the Johannine community in contrast to those who do not believe in Jesus, the Logos.   It is to be indicated that the "will of the flesh" cannot be confused with the flesh itself.   The community members are also born of the flesh.   In this regard, believers and disbelievers are exactly the same.   This is the reason why John employs the phrase, "nor of the will of the flesh" instead of "nor of the flesh."   If John had described that believers are born "not of flesh," he would have made a great mistake, since they also have had the flesh.   The believers, however, unlike the unbelievers, sees the supernatural origin in their fleshes.   They think that natural birth is not enough, and it is useless if it has not contained the divinity.   Thus, verse 13 is introduced to contrast the supernatural origin with the worldly origin.   R. E. Brown, on this, properly presents that

> "flesh" here is not a wicked principle opposed to God. Rather, it is the sphere of the natural, the powerless, the superficial, opposed to "spirit," which is the sphere of the heavenly and the real.[51]

Schnackenburg finds another point in verse 13.   According to him,

> the consciousness of belonging to God and being born of God characterizes 'Johannine' Christianity and gives it the certainty of being superior to the world.[52]

---

50. George R. Beasley-Murray, *John*, p.13.
51. R. E. Brown, *John*, I, p.12.

These scholars' indications are satisfactory as far as the contrast in verse 13 is concerned. What has been lacked in these indications, however, is the absence of another dimension that the believers' consciousness of belonging to God are not outside their flesh, but within the flesh. This point is often disregarded.

The birth in verse 13, of course, does not denote that "there existed a number of persons born in the manner described who in virtue of their birth were able to receive Christ when he came," as C. K. Barrett articulates.[53] Rather, it emphasizes that this birth is dependent on believing in Jesus the Logos. After believing in Jesus' name, the members of the community began to be convinced that they came from heaven. They think that they were in heaven before they are born of flesh on earth. As Jesus' heavenly state and earthly state are distinguished in the sense that the former has divinity only, while the latter both divinity and humanity(flesh), the community member's heavenly state and earthly state are to be discerned in the exactly same sense. When they were in heaven, they were in the level of divinity in the spirit, but now on earth they are degraded to the level of both divinity and humanity, or more precisely, the level of divinity within the flesh. The inclusive level of both divinity and humanity is less than the exclusive level of the divinity, as it was indicated before. In this regard, the community members forfeited their former glory in the level of exclusive divine status when they were born of flesh on earth, even though they retain the divinity at least in the flesh.

Believers less great than Jesus

John presents the community members as being less great

---

52. R Schnackenburg, *John*, I, p.263.
53. C. K. Barrett, *John*, p.164.

than Jesus. They are less than him, since their status of "the children of God" is solely dependent on Jesus. If they do not "receive" him, and do not "believe in his name," they cannot become "the children of God"(1.12).

The subordination of the believers to Jesus in another dimension is manifested in 14.12-24. They will be loved by Jesus and the Father, only if they should love Jesus and keep his commandments(14.21). D. Bruce Woll remarks clearly that

> belief in Jesus, in John's Gospel, means recognition that Jesus is the exclusive and pre-eminent authority.... The successor is one who believes in Jesus, and loves him, demonstrating his love by keeping his commandments. Four times from vs.15-24 the author reiterates the fact that the successor-agent is the one who loves Jesus in the sense of keeping his word or his commandments. The word *terein...* has not only the sense of "obey," but also the sense of submission to and preservation of a tradition.[54]

Although Woll's identification of John's adversary with the community's charismatic leaders, who upgrade dangerously their rank to Jesus is less than satisfactory, his emphasis on the difference between the agent and successor appears to be valid. The statement in 14.26 is to be also illuminated in terms of the submission of the believers to Jesus: "he [the Paraclete] will teach you all things, and bring to your remembrance all that I have said to you." The believers teach nothing new. They can only teach what Jesus have taught them. Furthermore, It is not the believers but the Paraclete who teaches.

Yet another aspect of the believers' submission to Jesus is disclosed in the following statements: "If you abide in my

---

54. D. Bruce Woll, *Johannine Christianity in Conflict: Authority, Rank, and Succession in the First Farewell Discourse* (Chico: Scholars Press, 1981), p.92.

word, you are truly my disciples"(8.31); "If you abide in me, and my words abide in you, ask whatever you will, and it shall be done for you"(15.7); "whoever hears my word ... has eternal life"(5.24). John could substitute "several nouns for logos without change in meaning, for example, voice, command, witness."[55] There is a close correlation between abiding in "me" and abiding in "my word(s)." The community members are not to abide directly in Jesus but only through his word. Paul S. Minear articulates that

> yet where that word is heard, there Jesus is present. This distinction is highly relevant to both the narrator and his readers, because they had not seen Jesus himself before his death and because their only access to him now is by listening to his word as it is being mediated through someone else. This fact helps to explain why John placed such a heavy emphasis on hearing this word.[56]

Minear's explanation is quite convincing. What has been lacked in this explanation, however is a reading so as to demonstrate what John in fact did want to reveal. In other words, the sociological implication concealed in John's statements is to be explored. In these statements John emphasizes insinuately on the difference between Jesus and his believers in terms of the latter's dependence on the former. The formulas, "If you" and "whoever," present the condition definitely. If the condition is not accomplished, they are not "truly his disciples," (8.31) what they ask shall not "be done for them"(15.7), and they cannot have "eternal life"(5.24). This condition reflects the social situation that the community tries to revise and to counteract the misunderstanding of those who upgrade themselves to equal standing with Jesus.

John emphasizes on the dependence of the believers on

---

55. P. S. Minear, *John. The Martyr's Gospel*, p.94.
56. *Ibid.*, 95.

Jesus. They are less great than Jesus. Jesus "sent them into the world" as the Father did(17.18). The Johannine Jesus addresses the statement, "nor is he who is sent greater than he who sent him"(13.16). The achievement of believers' recovery of their former divine glory depends on Jesus' praying for them(17.9), and on Jesus' approval. "The glory which you have given me I have given to them"(17.22). Without Jesus' giving activity they cannot receive the glory.

CHAPTER II

STRUGGLE FOR GLORY

CHAPTER II
STRUGGLE FOR GLORY

1. Jesus' Struggle for Glory

The Johannine Jesus begins to try to move toward the former exclusive status of divinity from the present inclusive status both of divinity and humanity. Jesus forfeited the status of God who has only divinity when he descended from heaven onto earth. But he retains his divinity in his flesh. Jesus' struggle to demonstrate his former divine status and the present divinity in his flesh is predominantly disclosed in his works and in his disputes against the Jews who charge that he is mere human. The Jews reject not only Jesus' former divinity with God but his present divinity in the flesh as well.

Glory manifested in works

John uses the term "work"(*ergon*) predominantly to denote Jesus' miracles, although the concept of miracle is narrower than that of "work," since the latter includes "words" also. Similarly, John reserves the term "sign"(*sēmeion*) for miracles, even as the concept of miracle is narrower than that of "sign," since the latter contains even non-miraculous event such as the cleansing of the temple(2.13-22). What is the relationship between "work" and "sign?" Raymond E. Brown's analysis in this regard is persuasive and illuminating.

The two Johannine terms for miracles, "works" and "signs,"

share as a background the OT description of God who acts on behalf of man. While both *ergon* and *sēmeion* occur in LXX accounts of the Exodus, the Synoptic term *dynamis* is rare... The term "work" expresses more the divine perspective on what is accomplished, and so is a fitting description for Jesus himself to apply to the miracles. The term "sign" expresses the human psychological viewpoint, and is a fitting description for others to apply to the miracles of Jesus.[1]

The Johannine Jesus avoids the term "sign," instead, he prefers to use the term "works." By the use of the term "*ergon*" the Johannine Jesus consociates his ministry with the works of the Father in the past: "My Father works until now, and I work"(5.17). This verse implies a close association between Jesus and the Father in their works.

The Johannine Jesus disclosed his divinity in seven signs. At the end of the story of the water changed into wine at Cana John adds his comment on this incident: "This, the first of his signs, Jesus did at Cana in Galilee, and he manifested his glory and his disciples believed in him"(1.11). How did the incident manifest the glory of Jesus? R. E. Brown answers this question in relation to the theme of replacement of Jewish institutions and religious views.

In view of this consistent theme of replacement, it seems obvious that, in introducing Cana as the first in a series of signs to follow, the evangelist intends to call attention to the replacement of the water prescribed for Jewish purification by the choicest of wines. This replacement is a sign of who Jesus is, namely, the one sent by the Father who is now the only way to the Father. All previous religious institutions, customs and feasts lose meaning in his presence.[2]

The meaning of this first sign, however, is not confined to

---

1. R. E. Brown, *John*, I , p.529.
2. R. E. Brown, *John*, I , p.104.

this sort of replacement, since this replacement is possible without the allusion to the glory of Jesus. For example, John portrays Jesus as the real temple(2.21). The Spirit he gives will replace the necessity of worshiping at Jerusalem(4.20-24). However, these portrayals of Jesus with the color of replacement are presented by John without any indications of Jesus' glory. This does not necessarily mean that the first sign does not convey the theme of replacement. Rather, it means that in the first sign, another replacement, apart from the replacement mentioned by Brown, is contained to reveal Jesus' glory. In what way did this first sign make Jesus' glory shine forth? Jeremiah 31.10-12 and Isaiah 25.6-8 give a hint to this question.

> They shall come and sing aloud on the height of Zion, and they shall be radiant over the goodness of the Lord, over the grain, the wine, and the oil, and over the young of the flock and the herd; their life shall be like a watered garden, and they shall languish no more(Jer.31.12).

> On this mountain the Lord of hosts will make for all people a feast of fat things, a feast of wine on the lees, of fat things full of marrow, of wine on the lees well refined... He will swallow up death for ever, and the Lord God will wipe away tears from all faces, and the reproach of his people he will take away from all the earth; for the Lord has spoken (Isa.25.6,8).

According to Jewish tradition the new wine of the New Age is provided only on the table of the eschatological meal. The Johannine Jesus, however, provides the best wine now, and in so doing Jesus is regarded as the one who is equal to God, the Master of history. H. C. Kee articulates, on this, explicitly.

> He brings the best wine(=eschatological joy) now. One need not wait until the End of the Age; the goal of history is already present in Jesus.[3]

The trumpet sounds already to announce the beginning of the New Age. Thus, the first sign replaces, above all, the traditional notion of the New Age. In Jewish tradition, only God brings the New Age in the future. In the first sign, the Johannine Jesus takes the role of God, and initiates the New Age in the present. This is the reason why John adds his comment on Jesus' glory to the story. The first sign reveals and stresses the divinity in the flesh of Jesus.

The story of the healing of the officer's son(4.46-53) also illuminates Jesus' divinity. G. R. Beasley-Murray's comment on it is quite obvious.

> The clue to the Evangelist's purpose in the narrative, its "sign" value, lies in the threefold reference to the statement of Jesus to the officer: *ho hyios sou zē*, "your son lives"(vv 50,51,53). The healing of the boy is a sign of the power of Jesus to give life, which in the discourse that follows will be defined as "eternal life"(5.24), and even life from the dead, resurrection life(5.21, 25-26, 28-29).[4]

Similarly, the story of the healing of the lame man at Bethesda(5.1-9b) is a sign that Jesus has the life-giving power to bring restoration to the man's health.

The story of the feeding of the five thousand(6.1-15) sets forth an understanding of Jesus as food that the Father, not Moses, provides to feed his own people: "it was not Moses who gave you the bread from heaven; my Father gives you the true bread from heaven. For the bread of God is that which comes down from heaven, and gives life to the world" (6.32-33). When the people saw the sign which fed the five thousand, they said "This is indeed the prophet who is to

3. H. C. Kee, *Jesus in History. An Approach to the Study of the Gospels*, 2nd ed.(New York: Harcourt Brace Jovanovich, Inc., 1977), p.221f.

4. G. R. Beasley-Murray, *John*, p.73.

come into the world!"(v.14). Jesus withdrew again to the hills by himself, when he perceived that the people were about to take him by force to make him king(v.15). Gerard Sloyan maintains, on verse 14, that

> Jesus has performed a genuine "sign" and the "people"... respond to it by acknowledging him as "the prophet"(cf.1:21) who "comes into the world." The latter is an important Johannine phrase(cf. 1:19; 3:19; 9:39; 11:27; 12:46; 16:28; 18:37). This acknowledgment on their part of Jesus' status as that of one who comes to prophesy, that is, to teach in God's name, is for John the sole appropriate response to the sign.[5]

Sloyan's argument is highly questionable. Two points may be indicated. 1. Sloyan fails to recognize a link between v.14 and v.15. The word "therefore"(*oun*) in v.15 denotes continuation of the statement in v.14. Jesus departed again(*palin*) to the hills because he had perceived people's acknowledgments of him not only as "king"(v.15) but as "prophet"(v.14) as well. Thus, Sloyan's explanation that the acknowledgment of Jesus as the "prophet" is "for John the sole appropriate response to the sign" seems to be indefensible. 2. According to Sloyan, the phrase "comes into the world," is "an important Johannine phrase." Undoubtedly, it is important in many other verses. But the phrase in this verse 14, contrary to Sloyan, is negatively introduced by John. John underestimates acknowledgment by the people of Jesus as one who only "comes into the world." They failed to recognize Jesus' divine origin of heavenly status, but rather only recognize his present visibility. They did not understand Jesus as the Son of God who "comes into the world." Their understanding of him is confined to "prophet" who "comes into the world." The interpretation of the phrase "comes into the world" is dependent on its context.

---

5. Gerard Sloyan, *John*(Atlanta: John Knox Press, 1988), p.65.

John also rejects the multitude's notion of Jesus as king who feeds his own people.

> Jesus' refusal to accede to the multitude's demands must be reckoned as one of the turning points in his ministry, for from this time Jesus and the crowds parted company.[6]

The political kingship is in contrast with the spiritual kingship which comes from above. The Johannine Jesus discloses this explicitly in the trial before Pilate: "My kingship is not of this world... my kingship is not from the world"(18.36). John tries to exhibit not Jesus' identity of prophet or king, but his divine identity in the story of the feeding of the five thousand. In the story of walking on the water(6.16-21) John reports Jesus' declaration: "I am"(6.20). The phrase, *ego eimi* ("I am") denotes another dimension of the manifestation of God in Jesus.

In the story of the healing of the man born blind(9.1-41)[7] Jesus commands the blind "to go, wash in the pool of Siloam (which means sent)"(9.7). Bruce Grigsby's argument on this is persuasive.

> Like the living waters throughout the Fourth Gospel, the waters of Siloam are dispensed by and through Christ. ... the pool of Siloam becomes for him [John] and his readership the pool of "he who is sent"(*apestalmenos*). And, of course, ... "he who is sent" is a frequent Messianic construct applied to Christ.[8]

---

6. G. R. Beasley-Murray, *John*, p.88.

7. J. M. Lieu proposes that "it was not the experience of becoming 'excluded from the synagogue' which prompted the development of the theology of 'being blinded'" in chapter 9. For detailed reason for it, see "Blindness in the Johannine Tradition," *NTS* 34(1988): 83-95, esp. 90.

8. B. Grigsby, "Washing in the Pool of Siloam – A Thematic Anticipation of the Johannine Cross," *Nov Test* 27(3, 1985): 227-235, quoted from 233f.

The meaning of the story, however, goes far beyond this. In the story, symbol of light is emphasized. As John Painter notes, light had become a symbol for the Law in the Jewish tradition. Here "John contends that Jesus, not the Law, gives man sight, perception, light, understanding and life."[9] In addition to it, the Johannine Jesus announces that his coming means a judgment: "For judgment I came into this world, that those who do not see may see, and that those who see may become blind"(v.39). This announcement can be reconciled with 3.17 which says "God sent the Son into the world, not to judge the world, but that the world might be saved through him," since, as R. Schnackenburg proposes, 3.17 is

> intended to highlight God's saving purpose. If anyone rejects the one sent by God, their unbelief becomes a judgment on them through their own guilt(3:18b; 12:48).[10]

In this story Jesus is viewed as the Judge of the world. In the Jewish tradition only God is the Judge of the world. Thus again, the divine power in Jesus is emphasized.

The story of Lazarus being raised from the dead(John 11) reveals Jesus' divine power to restore life or to give eternal life. Jesus is "the resurrection and the life"(v.25). This incident gives Jesus an opportunity to be glorified(v.4). Through this incident the Johannine Jesus tries to make "the people standing by" believe that he is sent by God(11.42). To believe this is to recognize Jesus' divinity.

The Johannine Jesus puts a statement, "for your sake I am glad that I was not there, so that you may believe"(v.15). On this, as Ernst Haenchen notes, here

---

9. John Painter, "John 9 and the Interpretation of the Fourth Gospel," *JSNT* 28 (1986): 31-61, esp. 56.

10. R. Schnackenburg, *The Gospel According to St John*, vol. II (New York: The Crossroad Publishing Company, 1982), p.255.

the narrator is convinced that the eyewitness to a resurrection
will come more readily to faith than the witness of a mere
healing. For the christology of the narrator the miraculous
deeds of Jesus are demonstrations of power that provide his
divine sonship. …The realm of the Father is "entirely other."
For that reason, miracles can only be pointers to what is
"entirely other."[11]

Despite his persuasive note cited above, Haenchen is only
partially correct when he goes one step further.

Here, in the case of the resurrection of Lazarus, the true
meaning concerns the resurrection of the spiritually dead to
fellowship with God, to authentic life.[12]

The story of the raising of Lazarus symbolizes not only "the
resurrection of the spiritually dead" but the resurrection of the
physically dead, since the physical state of Lazarus is
definitely described here: "by this time there will be an odor,
for he has been dead four days"(v.39). This story exhibits
Jesus' divine power which controls even the spiritual and
physical death, the final enemy of humans.[13]

Although the term *doxa* appears only 3 times in two
signs(2.11; 11.4,40), the Johannine Jesus manifested his *doxa*
through all the signs he did. The glory and signs are closely
interrelated. As W. Nicol has put it, the glory

is connected to the miracles… the glory is partly the
miraculous power as such. The voice from heaven in 12:28

---

11. Ernst Haenchen, *John* II (Philadelphia : Fortress Press, 1984),
p.60.

12. *Ibid.*, p.60.

13. For a recent study on the Lazarus story with the use of
modern rhetorical criticism, see Wilhelm Wuellner, "Putting Life Back
into the Lazarus Story and Its Reading: The Narrative Rhetoric of
John 11 as the Narration of Faith," *Semeia* 53(1991): 113-132.

may be taken to mean just what it says: "I have glorified it(my name), and I will glorify it again," i.e., glory *was* revealed in the earthly life of Jesus and will be revealed at his departure.[14]

Jesus manifested his glory in various signs through his flesh, e.g., his earthly life. But the glory of Jesus is not confined to signs. His glory encompasses much more than miraculous power. The miraculous power is included in his glory, but not *vice versa*. The glory "was revealed in the earthly life of Jesus," as W. Nicol notes, but we must ask further. Why did Jesus reveal the glory? The answer is that Jesus revealed it in order to restore and declare his divinity. All signs Jesus did in John are to be viewed in terms of his struggles to restore his exclusive former divinity (without flesh) forfeited now and to declare his present divinity retained in the flesh.

Dispute against the Jews

In the prologue, John presents a Moses-Jesus dichotomy (1.17). Moses the lawgiver is contrasted with Jesus the gracegiver. This proclivity runs throughout the Gospel. Moses-Jesus dichotomy is followed by the statement, "no one has ever seen God; it is God the only one, ever in the Father's bosom, who has revealed him"(1.18). It is W. H. Kelber who grasps quite clearly the constrast between Moses and Jesus in v.18.

> ...the polemical edge, "no one has ever seen God," is in part at least directed at Moses. But it is not Moses the lawgiver who is contrasted with the Logos, but Moses the visionary who on Sinai was in the presence of God(Exod 24:9-11; 33:18-23). Implied in these last verses is the understanding

---

14. W. Nicol, *The Sēmeia in the Fourth Gospel*(Leiden: E. J. Brill, 1972), p.133.

that Moses ascended and brought back the Law, without ever having seen, while the *Logos* who had "seen," descended and revealed what he had "seen."[15]

Kelber argues that John presents Moses as the lawgiver in v.17, but he regards insinuately Moses as the visionary in v.18, and that verse 18 declares Jesus' authority for the exclusive prestige of seeing God. Kelber is convincing when he explores the Johannine polemic against Moses in v.18, but the Exodus 24.9-11 he presented is not proper evidence for his argument. For in Exodus 24.9-11 Moses, with others, saw God: "Then Moses and Aaron, Nadab, and Abihu, and seventy of the elders of Israel went up, and they saw the God of Israel; ... they beheld God, and ate and drank." Was it really God that Moses and others saw? W. A. Meeks' note on this is highly plausible.

> The solution that emerges in later Jewish exegetical literature assumes that Scripture's visionaries did not really see God. What they saw must, therefore, have been some intermediary, either a representative or a representation of God. ....In Gen 1:26 God speaks of "our image" and "our likeness." And in Exod 23:21 God tells Moses of the angel who would accompany the Israelites: "My name is in him." What Israel's prophets saw was thus either God's image... or that highest angel who bore God's name, whom later mystics and exegetes would call "the lesser YHWH."[16]

Thus what is contrasted in v.18, unlike Kelber, is not between "without having seen" and "having seen," but between levels of "having seen." What Moses saw was not God but "a

---

15. W. H. Kelber, "The Birth of A Beginning: John 1:1-18," 139.

16. W. A. Meeks, "Equal to God," in *The Conversation Continues-Studies in Paul and John. In Honor of J. Louis Martyn*, ed. Robert T. Fortna and Beverly R. Gaventa(Nashville: Abingdon Press, 1990), pp.309-321, quoted from p.317f.

representative of a representation of God," while the only Son
saw the very presence of God. To make the latter disclose
clearly John inserts the phrase, "in the bosom of the Father."
John states that Jesus supersedes Moses in the sense that
Jesus is the exclusive Son who is regarded as the only
exception to the phrase, "no one has ever seen God." The
thought postured in 1.18 reappears more clearly in 6.46: "Not
that any one has seen the Father except him who is from
God; he has seen the Father."

John presents numerous polemics of Jesus against the Jews.
The purpose of these polemics is to reveal both the former
divine status of Jesus who was in the bosom of the Father,
and the present divinity retained in his earthly life. In the
cleansing of the temple in Jerusalem(2.13–22), disputing
against the Jews, the Johannine Jesus spoke of "the temple of
his body"(2.21). Jesus is regarded here as the place where
"God is to be adored, the true 'house of God'... With him
and in him the time of worship of God 'in spirit and truth'
(4.23) has dawned. His body is the source of the waters of
life."[17]

The violation of the Sabbath makes the Jews "persecute
Jesus"(5.16). The Johannine Jesus responds to them with the
statement, "My Father is working still, and I am working"
(5.17). Here Jesus is delineated as making "claims tantamount
to divinity."[18] Jesus proclaims that he is doing only what he
sees the Father doing(5.19). The Father and the Son are the
same in regard to raising the dead and giving them life(5.21),
but the activity of judgment is the exclusive possession of the
Son(5.22). What does Jesus' activity on the Sabbath reflect?
Indeed God does not cease to work on the Sabbath. Humans
are born and die on the Sabbath. This means God remains
active on the Sabbath, since only God can give life and pass

---

17. R. Schnackenburg, *John,* II, p.352.
18. R. E. Brown, *John,* I , p.216.

it away. Thus Jesus' activity on the Sabbath exhibits his equality to God, since for the Jews "the Sabbath privilege was peculiar to God, and no one was equal to God(Exod xv 11; Isa xlvi 5; Ps lxxxix 8)."[19] To declare the right to work even on the Sabbath is to declare his former divine status and the present divinity retained in the fleshy life.

The Johannine Jesus reveals himself as the real bread of life(6.35,48). The bread of God comes down from heaven(6.33). But it was not Moses but the Father who gave the people the true bread from heaven(6.32). Jesus claims to be the bread which initiates and sustains life. Murmuring at Jesus the Jews hesitate to accept his claim(6.41f.). Murmuring was a typical trait of the Jews in their wandering period. They murmured about the lack of water(Exod. 15.24) and of bread(Exod.16.2). The Jews make an objection against Jesus' claim to be the bread that comes down from heaven, since they are convinced that Jesus is the son of Joseph(6.42). However, as G. R. Beasley-Murray notes, "the feature of 'bread' is not at this point contested; it is the claim to have come down 'from heaven' that appears impossible."[20]

Jesus supersedes the fathers of Israel who "ate the manna in the wilderness and died"(6.49), since he is the living bread(6.51) come down "from heaven," that a man may eat of it and not die(6.50). R. Schnackenburg articulates properly in this regard that

> it is striking that death of the fathers in wilderness is strongly emphasized. This negative event throws into sharper contrast the promise of the life the true bread which comes down from heaven can give. In addition it is meant to warn the Jews as they mutter in unbelief that they could suffer a similar fate to their fathers.[21]

---

19. R. E. Brown, *John*, I , p.217.
20. G. R. Beasley-Murray, *John*, p.93.
21. R. Schnackenburg, *John*, II , p.54.

Eating of this living bread, which preserves life, is here such that it really overcomes death. The Johannine Jesus tries to make the Jews recognize his heavenly origin here. Numerous uses of *ego eimi*(6.35,41,48,51) are presented to confirm his divine origin. They should see his divinity in his flesh given "for the life of the world"(6.51).

Jesus' response to the objection of the Jews(6.52) is deliberately sharp. Unless anyone eats the flesh of the Son of Man and drink his blood, they have no life in themselves (6.53). Anyone who wants to abide in Jesus must eat his flesh and drink his blood(6.56). The term, "eat"(trōgein) "does not have to be understood in an extreme realistic sense ('chew')."[22] John presents here "the symbolic eating of the heavenly bread."[23] The evangelist emphasizes again on Jesus' divine origin. Jesus has been sent by "the living Father"(6.57). He lives through the Father(6.57). Anyone who wants to live through him must eat him.

Why does John stress eating of Jesus' flesh which he regards as the bread of life come down from heaven? The answer is to be sought in terms of John's argument against those who admit Jesus' flesh(the son of Joseph) while rejecting his divine origin. They judge "according to the flesh"(8.15). John accepts their admission of the flesh, but he counteracts their narrow sense of the flesh, and gives a deep implication to it. John emphasizes that unlike the other ordinary fleshes, Jesus' flesh which contains the divinity is not to be disregarded. Jesus' flesh is the living bread come down from heaven. Unless they recognize and believe in the divinity in the flesh of Jesus, they preserve no life in themselves.

The Jews charge Jesus with the remark that he can hardly know the scriptures since he is not educated(7.15). Jesus

---

22. *Ibid.*, p.62.
23. *Ibid.*, p.62.

responds to them with the statement, "My teaching is not mine, but his who sent me"(7.16). Jesus defends himself "by pointing to his teaching, which bears within itself the signs of its divine origin."[24] In the Jewish tradition, the route to teaching the word of God was through Scripture. The Scripture was seen as the sole way to mediate between humans and God. But Jesus is directly teaching without the mediation of the word of God. He speaks as the Father taught him(8.28). John emphasizes again on the divine origin of Jesus. Jesus knows whence he has come and whither he is going, while the Pharisees do not know whence Jesus comes or whither he is going(8.14). The Johannine Jesus argues that he came forth from God(8.42).

The Johannine Jesus pronounces that he came into the world to make the blind see, and those who see blind(9.39). The Pharisees raise an objection to this pronouncement. E. Haenchen paraphrases Jesus' answer(9.41) to this objection as follows.

> Because you claim that you see, that is, that you know God, and do not recognize him, for you there is no forgiveness of sin.[25]

Some of this paraphrasing is to be supplemented or more clarified with the phrase, "do not recognize Him within me," instead of "do not recognize him." If Jesus "was not from God he could do nothing"(9.33). Unless the Pharisees see his divine origin, their guilt remains(9.41).

2. The Community's Struggle for Glory

Greater works than these

---

24. *Ibid.*, p.132.
25. E. Haenchen, *John*, II, p.41.

One of the most ambiguous verses in John is 14.12: "truly, truly, I say to you, one who believes (*ho pisteuōn*) in me will do (*poiēsei*) the works that I do; indeed, one will do (*poiēsei*) greater works than these, because I am going to the Father." Three questions are to be raised here. 1. Who is "ho pisteuōn"? 2. What is the purpose of John's introducing of this verse? 3. What is the content of "greater works"?

Who is *"ho pisteuōn"*? Who are the subjects to perform "greater works"? Most scholars such as C. K. Barrett, R. Schnackenburg, and R. E. Brown presuppose that they are the disciples.[26] D. B. Woll takes the same position in this regard. According to Woll,

> when Jesus goes away, the believer will take the place of Jesus as agent of the works Jesus has been doing. The stature of the disciples as successor-agents of the works of Jesus is underscored by the promise that the disciples will do "greater" works than those Jesus has done.[27]

Not only Woll's argument, but those of the other scholars mentioned above are far from obvious. John distinguishes between "you" in the initial rhetoric and "one who believes." The former is presented in plural form, while the latter in sigular form. From the time of the evangelist, "you" denotes Jewish Christians whose place is in the apostolic tradition, while "one who believes" the members of the Johannine community.

The presupposition that the community members, who are vehemently competing against the Jewish Christians of the

---

26. C. K. Barrett, *John.* p.460; R. Schnackenburg, *The Gospel According to St John,* vol. III(New York: The Crossroad Publishing Company, 1982), pp.71-72; R. E. Brown, *The Gospel According to John,* vol. II(New York: Doubleday & Company Inc., 1970), p.633.

27. D. B. Woll, *Johannine Christianity in Conflict,* p.80f.

apostolic trajectory, regard the subjects to perform the "greater works" as the Jewish Christian cannot be sustained. In verse 11, the disciples are admonished to believe Jesus twice. In other words, they are counted now to be non-believers in a strict sense or at least improper believers. Woll and others mentioned above seem to fail to grasp this point. It is not plausible that the so-called "non-believers," who do not "believe" in a certain aspect of Jesus in v.11, become suddenly the "one who believes" in v.12 without any explanation. What I wish to argue here is that the subjects to perform the "greater works" are not the disciples or Jewish Christians who stand up in the apostolic line, but the members of the Johannine community whose position is in sharp contrast to the disciples.

In this sense C. Dietzfelbinger's argument that verse 12 reflects a self-understanding of the Johannine community is manifestly compelling.[28] But his other argument that verse 12 is the "aktualisierende Interpretation" of 5.20f[29] is less convincing, since there is a gulf between 14.12 and 5.20f. In the former the subjects to perform the greater works are the believers, while in the latter the subject to show the greater works is the Father.

What is the purpose of John's introducing of this verse? First of all, the question of when the believer performs the greater works is to be answered. The believer "will perform" it. But when does this performance occur? Will it be in the future or in the present? R. E. Brown emphasizes the "eschatological character" of the greater works.[30] However, he does not set the time of the performance. The future tense in the phrase ("will perform") is the present, if we see it from John's time. D. B. Woll

---

28. C. Dietzfelbinger, "Die Größeren Werke (John 14:12f)," *NTS* 35(1989): 27-47. esp.27.

29. *Ibid.*, 32.

30. R. E. Brown, *John*, II, p.633.

seems to fail to see this point when he argues as follows.

> Where vss.4–11 were cast in the present tense and had to do
> with the response of the disciples to Jesus and the Father...
> 12–17 return to the future tense and have to do with the
> future activity and authority of the disciples. Formally, vss.
> 4–11 are an exhortation to believe, whereas vss.12–17 are a
> promise, almost an investiture.[31]

Two points of Woll's arguments are to be modified: "the
future" activity is the present activity in John's eyes; the
authority of "the disciples" is to be replaced by the authority
of the Johannine community.

The verse reflects the social situation of the Johannine
community since it discloses clearly that "Jesus' return to the
Father is the condition of performing these works."[32] The
community members think that their activity is far beyond
that of the Jewish Christians who place themselves in the
apostolic tradition. In other words, this verse 12 emphasizes
that the activity of the past disciples through the earthly
Jesus is less than the activity of the present community
members through the heavenly Jesus. This verse, thus,
reduces and minimizes the significance of the activity of the
Jewish Christians whose present authority is dependent on the
past apostles.

What is the content of "greater works"? On this, C. K.
Barrett proposes that

> the greater works therefore are the gathering of many converts
> into the church through the activity of the disciples (cf. 17.20;
> 20.29).[33]

---

31. D. B. Woll, *Johannine Christianity in Conflict*, p.81.
32. G. Sloyan, *John*, p.180.
33. C. K. Barrett, *John*, p.460.

Barrett regards the greater works as the numerical enlargement of new converts. R. Schnackenburg hesitates to accept this sort of interpretation.

> These 'greater works' can... justifiably be applied to the missionary successes of the disciples. If, however, we are to preserve the full meaning intended by the evangelist, we must be on our guard against a purely external view, since the 'greater' works were not for him external expansion and successes... but the increasing flow of God's power into man's world(17:12), the gathering together of God's scattered children(11:52) and the judgment of the unbelieving world (see 16:8-11). This cannot be done until Jesus' exaltation (12:31f), his departure to the Father.[34]

I do agree with Schnackenburg's hesitation. Nevertheless, his suggestion remains unproved also. For if the contents of the verses he presented are applied to the Johannine community, they merely show the similar activities that Jesus did, not the greater works than these. R. E. Brown presents another suggestion.

> After Jesus has been glorified (xvii 1,5), the Father will perform in His Son's name works capable of manifesting the Son's glory... There was another reference to "greater works" in v.20... in a context referring to judging and giving life, and perhaps a share in these two works is included in what the disciples are now being promised.[35]

Brown does not clarify the content of "greater works" here. He alludes only that the greater works may be similar to those postured in 5.20. This allusion, however, is less persuasive. For judging and giving life are works Jesus

---

34. R. Schnackenburg, *John*, III, p.72.
35. R. E. Brown, *John*, II, p.633.

performed already, as 5.21-22 irradiates. It is declared that the purpose of Jesus' coming into this world is for judgment (9.39). Furthermore, Jesus is reported to have raised the dead Lazarus(11.43-44). If the believers perform such works, it is not the "greater" works than these, but the "similar" works to these. But it is the "greater" works than these that the believers are promised. John does not disclose the content of the greater works in his gospel publicly. Nevertheless, the exegetes should not stop at this spot. They are requested to explore "the common assumptions that the writer shares with his reader concerning... the structure of their world."[36]

The greater works are to be illuminated in terms of revealing the divinity of the Johannine community as the divine circle of the "children of God." As the past Jesus did the works to reveal his divinity, so the present community members do the works to reveal his divinity. The community members, however, goes beyond these works. They perform the "greater works" which reveal not merely Jesus' divinity but their own divinities as well. Their performance of the "greater works" is to be viewed in terms of their struggle for the restoration of their glory forfeited in their present state.

Dispute against the Jewish Christians

The social context of the Johannine community is reflected more clearly in the farewell discourses(13.31-17.26) than any other passages of John.[37] The farewell discourses exhibit distinctly the community's dispute against the apostolic Jewish Christians who have their place and authority in the

---

36. H. C. Kee, *Community of the New Age. Studies in Mark's Gospel* (Philadelphia: The Westminster Press, 1977), p.50.

37. For the exploration in the farewell discourses in terms of the Jewish farewell speeches, see Ernst Bammel, "Die Abschiedsrede des Johannesevangeliums und Ihr Jüdischer Hintergrund," *Neotestamentica* 26(1, 1992): 1-12.

apostolic trajectory. Some scholars have utilized Mary Douglas' group/grid model[38] to analyze the features of the Johannine community. According to J. H. Neyrey, the farewell discourses reflect both a strong group/low grid and a weak group/low grid.[39]   W. R. Domeris argues that the farewell discourses disclose a strong group/low grid only.[40] J. A. Du Rand, on the other hand, suggests that the first farewell discourse, not the whole farewell discourses, exhibits a strong group/high grid.[41] According to Du Rand, the Johannine community

> with its strong group and grid features lives from their belief in Jesus, as the knowing pre-existent logos, in the self – understanding that they are the community of the Spirit of truth. And in this sense group in grid feeds each other. At the time of the First Farewell Discourse the Johannine community matched the C quadrant on Douglas's diagram.[42]

Mary Douglas' group/grid model shows nothing more than a general outlook of a given social unit. According to this model, all groups are to be simply classified into four types. This model does not properly analyze the social dynamics of

---

38. Group refers to the degree of societal pressure within a given social unit to conform to the society's norms, while grid the degree of socially constrained adherence of members of a group to the prevailing symbols and beliefs.

39. J. H. Neyrey, *An Ideology of Revolt. John's Christology in Social-Science Perspective* (Philadelphia: Fortress Press, 1988), pp.142-150.

40. W. R. Domeris, "The Farewell Discourse. An Anthropological Approach," *Neotestamentica* 25(1991): 233-250.

41. J. A. Du Rand, "A Story and A Community: Reading the First Farewell Discourse(John 13:31-14:31) From Narratological and Sociological Perspective," *Neotestamentica* 26(1992): 31-45, esp. 39-44.

42. *Ibid.*, 39f.

the very peculiar groups. Furthermore, neither the relationships between the four types, nor the social conditions moving from one type to another type are exhibited in the model. Only simple and hasty generalization of all given groups is elucidated in this model.

The farewell discourses reflect the Johannine community's polemic against the apostolic Jewish Christians whose theological position is grounded on the apostolic tradition. The past Jesus' polemics against the disciples signify the present community's disputes against the Jewish Christians. The apostolic Jewish Christians, whose representatives are symbolized as the twelve disciples, appear as one of the most prominent groups competing with the Johannine community. John tries to distinguish the positive aspects of the apostolic Jewish Christians and their negative aspects. He preserves the former and exhorts his community to adopt it. On the other hand, he rejects the latter and exhorts his community not to follow it.

The Johannine community and the apostolic Jewish Christians are in the "crisscrossing conflict"(L.A.Coser) in which someone who is an ally in one dispute is an opponent in another. Although the Johannine community conflicts with the apostolic Jewish Christians, the community cannot but admit that there are some common convictions between them. John allows some credit to the apostolic Jewish Christians in certain areas, though he bitterly denounces them in many other areas which include their limited understanding of Jesus and his glory. The community struggles to substitute its own christology for that of the apostolic Jewish Christians. The glory is given to the Johannine community, when its christology is accepted, while the christology of the apostolic Jewish Christians is rejected. The community is glorified when its understanding of Jesus and itself is recognized by the people as the supreme one. The community's dispute against the apostolic Jewish Christians is to be interpreted in terms of its struggle for the glory. The Johannine Jesus claims that

> I came from the Father and have come into the world; again,
> I am departing the world and going to the Father(16.28).

This claim forms one of the keynotes of John's Gospel. It reflects not merely John's view of Jesus, but the self-understanding of the Johannine community. The community members regard themselves as those who came from(*ek tou*,1.13; *para*,17.7) God, and who are going to Him. As Jesus came from God, so they came from God. As Jesus returned to heaven, so they will return to heaven(14.3). The community has recognized Jesus' former glory which he had with God "before the world was made"(17.5). In addition, the community has seen his glory manifested in the flesh(1.14), and will confirm his glory without the flesh in heaven(17.5,24). The community tries to convince the people of its divine origin, its present status as "children of God"(1.12), and of its future glory united with Jesus who is with God in heaven.

The introduction(13.31-32) of the first farewell discourse[43]

---

43. On the structure of the first farewell discourse, F. F. Segovia divides it into three parts: 13.31-38; 14.1-27; 14.28-31. Segovia, "The Structure, *Tendenz*, and *Sitz Im Leben* of John 13:31-14:31," *JBL* 104(3, 1985): 471-493. But the introduction is to be reduced to 13.31-32, since the insufficient understanding of the individual disciples appears in 13.33 on. D. B. Woll presents five divisions: 13.31-14.3; 14.4-11; 14.12-17; 14.18-24; 14.25-31. Woll, *Johannine Christianity in Conflict*, pp.12-31. Woll's division in regard to 13.31-14.3 is provocative, since it, along his thesis, disregards the traditional demarcation line between 13.38 and 14.1. But the title he gives to 14.4-11, "the concentration of authority in the Son," is too inclusive to summarize the unit, for such title can be applied not to the given unit but to the whole of the first farewell discourse. I presuppose three divisions: 13.31-32; 13.33-14.27; 14.28-31. Unlike Segovia and Woll, I set up 13.33-14.27 as the main body, since 13.31

portrays both the glory of Jesus and the glory of God through Jesus, and the glory of God and the glory of Jesus through God. The Johannine Jesus says to the disciples as he said to the Jews: "Where I am going you cannot come"(13.33). The Johannine Jesus here presupposes the distinction between the Jews and the disciples, and applies his criticism against the past Jews to the present disciples. In this sense F. F. Segovia's argument that the evangelist criticizes not the disciples but the Jews is far from obvious. According to Segovia,

> the proposed polemic may be clearly seen in the sharp and thorough differentiation elaborated within the discourse between the disciples and the Jews. This differentiation is at first presented indirectly in the introductory subsection of 13:31-38. Thus, after Jesus' departure, the situation of the disciples is described as being ultimately quite unlike that of the Jews: whereas the latter will not find Jesus(7.23-26) and will consequently die in their sin(8:21-24), the former... are promised, through Peter, that they will indeed follow Jesus at a later time.[44]

> In addition, all of subsequent promises made to the disciples in the discourse are also explicitly and repeatedly denied to "the world"(vv.17b-d, 18-20, 22, 27a-c), a category which in the light of 13:31-33 can only mean the Jews. The contrast is perhaps best summarized by the designation accorded to the disciples in the discourse: "little children"(13.13).[45]

I agree with Segovia that John differentiates between the

---

begins to disclose the critical proclivity to the disciples.

44. F. F. Segovia, "The Structure," 489.

45. F. F. Segovia, " 'Peace I Leave with You: My Peace I Give to You': Discipleship in the Fourth Gospel," in *Discipleship in the New Testament,* ed. F. F. Segovia (Philadelphia: Fortress Press, 1985), p.87f.

disciples and the Jews in the first farewell discourse, but I disagree with him in regard to the purpose of the differentiation. Unlike Segovia the purpose of it is not to criticize the Jews and protect the disciples. Rather, it is to shift the critical proclivity against the Jews to the disciples. In other words, the first farewell discourse exhibits clearly the deficiency of the disciples' understanding of Jesus and themselves.

The disciples, like the Jews, cannot follow where Jesus is going. The critical proclivity against the disciples is clearly manifested in Jesus' answer to Peter's question, "Lord, where are you going?"(13.36). Jesus answers, "Where I am going you cannot follow me now; but you shall follow afterward." Here "now"(*nun*) is contrasted to "afterward"(*hysteron*). This contrast appeared already in 13.7, "What I am doing you do not know yet, but later you will understand." Although here in 13.36 the different words are used, the contrasting proclivity is similar to 13.7. What do the words, "now" and "afterward" denote respectively? What does John emphasize through this contrast? C. K. Barrett's attempt typifies traditional interpretation.

> Peter is unwilling to abide by the distinction of 'now' and 'then', the eschatological distinction which for John is also a spiritual distinction... following Jesus... can take place only in a future guaranteed by the Spirit. Peter's intentions are excellent, but he remains within the world of sin, ignorance, and unbelief.[46]

Barrett's note that Peter remains "within the world of sin, ignorance, and unbelief" is convincing. His understanding, however, in regard to "now" and "then" in terms of "spiritual distinction" is less compelling. For the "now" is for John the past, while "then"("afterward") for him the present. Thus the

---

46. C. K. Barrett, *Jonh*, p.453.

distinction between the two is not the spiritual one, but the chronological one.

What does John intend through this chronological distinction? On this, D. B. Woll articulates as follows.

> There is, first of all, a distinction in the sequence or order of ascent to heaven. Jesus goes first. The disciples cannot follow until "afterwards" (13.36).[47]

> The delay in time between the ascent of Jesus and the subsequent ascent of the disciples expresses a difference in the heavenly status or rank of the disciples and Jesus, a difference between original and derived status.[48]

Woll's argument is original and persuasive. He extracts the temporal and spatial priority of Jesus over the disciples in this verse. This priority of Jesus, however, contrary to Woll, does not necessarily imply that John attacks against "the charismatic claimants" who try to abolish the distinction between Jesus and themselves. Rather, verse 36 reflects John's attack against poor discipleship of the apostolic Jewish Christians. Peter is forestalled to follow not "now," but "afterward." The "now" is the past for John's time, while "afterward" the present for him. This verse undermines the present following activity(expressed by "afterward") of the apostolic Jewish Christians whose authority is grounded on the past(expressed by "now") of the disciples whose main representative is Peter. John highlights the past of Peter. Peter was forestalled "not to follow" him in his time. John tries to weaken the foundation of the present discipleship of the apostolic Jewish Christians.

Peter declared that he will lay down his life for Jesus(v.37), but he was foretold by Jesus that he will deny him three

---

47. D. B. Woll, *Johannine Christianity in Conflict*, p.37f.
48. *Ibid.*, p.41.

times(v.38). This anticipation was realized in 18.17, 25-27. As spoken of the Jews, not only Peter(13.36,38) but the disciples(13.33) as well cannot follow Jesus. Thus, the verses (13.33,36,38) reflect the statement made to the Jews in 7.34: "You will seek me and you will not find me. Where I am you cannot come." In view of John's firm criticism against the Jews, this parallelism between the disciples or Peter and the Jews reflects the Johannine community's criticism against the negative aspect of the apostolic Jewish Christians. Peter did not understand the meaning of Jesus' departure to mean his entering into the sphere of glory. Peter's ignorance is compared with the Jews who neither understand nor recognize the glory of Jesus.

John denounces Peter in many other passages in his Gospel. Unlike the synoptic gospels, John does not introduce Peter as the first disciple of Jesus. Andrew, Peter's brother is a mediator between Jesus and Peter(1.40-42). Peter shows no significant response to Jesus in his initial encounter with him(1.42), although Jesus manifested the divine power to recognize Peter as "Simon the son of John" at his first glance.

According to John, Jesus has an initiative to choose the disciples. The Johannine Jesus announces that "You did not choose me, but I chose you and appointed you that you should go and bear fruit"(15.16). But Jesus does not exercise his initiative in choosing Peter. Rather, Peter comes first to Jesus without the latter's calling(1.42). This seems to arouse suspicion that Peter may not belong to "those whom Jesus chooses." Most scholars who participated in a scholastic meeting between Lutheran and Roman Catholic seem to have failed to grasp this point.[49] Besides Peter, Andrew who also comes to Jesus without the latter's calling(1.37,40) and who

---

49. R. E. Brown, K. P. Donfried, and J. Reumann, eds., *Peter in the New Testament*(New York: Paulist Press, 1973), p.131.

brings Peter to Jesus is not regarded as a prominent figure. Andrew appears two more times(6.8; 12.22) other than chater 1, but his role is trivial in both of them. Rather, Philip whom Jesus called with his own initiative is regarded as an outstanding figure. Philip appears eleven times in John. This reduces the role of Andrew, Peter's brother relatively. Later, Andrew hears Jesus' calling, "Come and see," and he comes and sees where Jesus is staying (1.39). Consequently, Andrew's response to Jesus is considered, in a certain sense, to supersede Peter who does not show any response in this scene.

Peter confesses Jesus as "the Holy One of God"(*ho hagios tou theou*) in 6.69. If this confession, is separated from its social context, it is to be considered as the significant one. The title, "the Holy One of God" appears only three times in the whole New Testament. Other than John, it appears in Mark 1.24 and Luke 4.34. In both cases, it comes from Satan. A. H. Maynard argues that Peter is not identified with Satan in this scene.[50] His argument, however, is to be regarded not to read the implication between the lines. Unlike the other gospels, John, of course, does not introduce Jesus' announcement which identifies Peter with Satan.[51] However, the primitive Christians intentionally avoided the title. It is not accidental that all appearances of the title in the New Testament, except John, are connected to Satan. The use of the title was very restrained in comparison to the other titles such as the Son of God, the Lord, and the Christ. John's linkage of the title with Peter means that Peter's activity is similar to Satan's activity.

This argument is reinforced by the following scene in which the Johannine Jesus does not confer any praise or authority to

---

50. A. H. Maynard, "The Role of Peter in the Fourth Gospel," *NTS* 30(1984): 532–548, esp. 534.

51. See Mk 8.33; Mt 16.23.

Peter, after the latter's confession. The Matthean Jesus does confer it to Peter: "Blessed are you, Simon... and on this rock I will build my church, and the power of death shall not prevail against it. I will give you the keys of the kingdom, and whatever you bind on earth shall be bound in heaven, and whatever you loose on earth shall be loosed in heaven" (Mt.16.17-19). The Johannine Jesus, however, does not comment on Peter's confession.

John exposes Peter's misunderstanding of Jesus' washing the disciples' feet in 13.6-17. Jesus shows a sacrificial model for love through this washing activity, but Peter adheres to the activity itself. E. L. Titus,[52] A. H. Maynard[53] and G. F. Snyder[54] display John's negative view of Peter. Especially Snyder explores John's critical view of Peter in 13.16 "nor is who is sent greater than he who sent him." Here "who is sent" is a translation of "*apostolos*." Thus, this verse denotes clearly that the apostle is not greater than Jesus. In this sense Snyder's argument that the Christianity originated not from the apostles but from the life of Jesus is provocative and convincing. But not only Titus and Maynard but Snyder failed to grasp that 13.7 was introduced by John to attack Peter. The Johannine Jesus said to Peter: "What I am doing you do not know now, but afterward you will understand." Here "now" is the past for John, while "afterward" the present for him. The apostolic Jewish Christians exercise their own authority from Peter who had a special relationship with the historical Jesus. John reminds them of the past Peter, their ideal leader. The past Peter did not even know what Jesus was doing. Although Peter worked with Jesus, he did not understand Jesus at that time. Thus, 13.7 is to be regarded as

---

52. E. L. Titus, *The Message of the Fourth Gospel*(New York: Abingdon, 1957), p.187.

53. A. H. Maynard, "The Role of Peter," 534f.

54. G. F. Snyder, "John 13:16 and the Anti-Petrinism of the Johannine Tradition," *BR* 16(1971): 5-15.

a fatal attack against the present would-be following of the apostolic Jewish Christians, since it undermines their foundation on Peter's past activity.

Peter is negatively assessed again by John in 18.10-11, where he, with a sword, struck the high priest's slave, and cut off his [Malchus] right ear. Jesus exhorts Peter to put his sword into its sheath. Why has John deliberately identified the man, who drew his sword, as Peter? Arthur J. Droge suggests a convincing and scrupulous exegesis on this passage.

> It is to reveal Peter as the disciple who is not a *hypēretēs* of Jesus. Admittedly, Peter fights to defend Jesus, but his action ... merits a harsh rebuke from his would-be master. Moreover, when Peter's desperate act is interpreted in light of Jesus' statement "If my kingdom were of this world, my subjects would fight"(18:36), it becomes clear that the author of the Fourth Gospel has leveled a devastating indictment at Peter. That Peter *does* fight suggests, at a minimum, that he has a fundamental misunderstanding of Jesus and of the nature of his kingship and kingdom. Worse still, Peter's action reveals that he is not a "subject" of Jesus' heavenly kingdom, and thereby confirms the truth of his "denial" of being Jesus' disciple.[55]

Jesus' advance notice on Peter's denial is actualized in 18.17-18, 25-27. Peter denies Jesus three times(18.17,25,27). Peter who once showed his loyalty to Jesus swearing that he will lay his life(13.37), dissociates himself from Jesus, and thereby keeps his life.

18.27 also exhibits a negative portrayal of Peter: "Peter again denied it; and at once the cock crowed." Mark reports Peter's weeping(Mk.14.72), Matthew and Luke report that Peter "wept bitterly"(Mt.26.75; Lk.22.62). Mark anticipates the

---

55. Arthur J. Droge, "The Status of Peter in the Fourth Gospel: A Note on John 18:10-11," *JBL* 109(2, 1990): 307-311, quoted from 311.

possibility of Peter's remedy passively, while Matthew and Luke anticipate it affirmatively. But John, unlike those authors, does not suggest the possibility of Peter's recovery. The Johannine Peter does neither "weep" nor "weep bitterly." Only the cock crows. John blocks up any expectations of Peter's restoration.

The denouncement of Peter's authority is still retained in 21.1-7. It was not Peter but the Beloved Disciple who recognized the resurrected Jesus first(21.7). Without the Beloved Disciple's indication, Peter would not perceive the resurrected Jesus. C. K. Barrett fails to recognize the deep meaning of this indication of the Beloved Disciple. According to him,

> seven disciples... *following the lead of Peter* determine to resume their work of fishing.[56]

Rather, Peter's authority is subordinated to the Beloved Disciple, as we indicated it above.

A. H. Maynard posits that Peter restores his authority in a high level in 21.8-14.

> I agree with such scholars as Bultmann, Barrett, Macgregor and Titus who see one of the major functions of this unit to be the restoration of Peter to primacy in the evangelistic and pastoral work of the Church.[57]

His position, however, is questionable. In 21.8-14 the Johannine Jesus speaks not to Peter privately, but to the whole "disciples." The restoration of Peter's authority is actualized with the restoration of the disciples as a whole. Thus, this unit rather weakens Peter's primacy and his representative role.

---

56. C. K. Barrett, *John*, p.577. Italics mine.
57. A. H. Maynard, "The Role of Peter," 541.

In 21.15–24 Peter is restored to a certain degree. Jesus gives him the pastoral authority but Peter's answer with "*phileō*," to Jesus' first and second questions with "*agapaō*" discloses that Peter did not clearly grasp the demand postured in Jesus' questions. Jesus' alteration of "*agapaō*" with "*phileō*" in his third question denotes his lessened expectation of Peter. In 21.7 John reports that Peter was "grieved." As Gilbert L. Bartholomew notes, "Peter's answers are moving from an initial shame at his denial of Jesus to a deepening shame that culminated in grief."[58] Thus the position that chapter 21 does not attack against Peter's pastoral authority[59] remains unproved. Instead, chapter 21 attacks Peter's authority partly and at the same time admits it in a certain degree.

The evangelist's last comment also functions as the fatal criticism against Peter: "This is the disciple who is bearing witness to these things; and who has written these things; and we know that his testimony is true"(21.24). This verse reveals the superiority of the Beloved Disciple over Peter, for it discloses that all works of Peter are dependent on the Beloved Disciple's witness and report. In other words, without the witness and report of the Beloved Disciple, even partial restoration of Peter is not to be accomplished.

Not only Peter but the other disciples are severely criticized by John. The Johannine Jesus addresses the disciples: "In my Father's house are many dwellings... when I go and prepare a place for you, I will come again and will take you to myself" (14.2–3). What is the meaning of "house"(*oikia*) and "dwellings"(*monai*) in it? According to G. R. Beasley–Murray,

> the Father's "house" with its many dwellings is most plausibly a pictorial representation of the transcendent dwelling

---

58. G. L. Bartholomew, "Feed My Lambs: John 21:15–19 As Oral Gospel," *Semeia* 39(1987): 69–96, esp. 69.

59. R. E. Brown, et al., *Peter*, p.147.

of God, such as is depicted under the figure of "the city of the living God, the heavenly Jerusalem" in Heb 12:22, a symbol which is greatly elaborated in the apocalyptic vision of the City of God in Rev 21:9–22:5.[60]

This interpretation appears to be invalid. What is the meaning of "house" in other passages in John? In 5.53 the "house" means not the building but the family. The same meaning can be attached to the "house" in 8.35. Thus, the "house" in 14.2 is to be regarded not as God's building but as His family.

The meaning of the "house" determines the meaning of "dwellings" whose equivalent is "place"(*topos*) in 14.3. The "dwellings" or "place" signifies not a geographical location, but a sphere. The Father's dwelling represents the sphere of glory. Jesus departs the earth to enter into the sphere of glory. He prepares an opportunity to participate in the sphere of glory for the disciples. In this sense, C. K. Barrett's note that "John... is not thinking of compartments or dwelling–places, but of the action, or state, of *menein*" appears to be valid.[61]

Robert H. Gundry interprets the dwellings as follows.

We are not at first to regard the "abodes" as rooms in heaven which are being constructed for us by the architect of the Celestial City. For throughout the Upper Room Discourse the leitmotif "abiding" is a present spiritual experience: "the Father... dwells in me"(14.10); "... He who abides in me, and I in him... If you abide in me, and my words abide in you..." (15.4–7).[62]

Gundry's proposition is highly defensible, if his restriction of "at first" is disregarded. In Gundry the proposition cited above

---

60. G. R. Beasley–Murray, *John*, p.249.
61. C. K. Barrett, *John*, p.457.
62. R. H. Gundry, "'In my Father's House are many *Monai*' (John 14.2)," *ZNW* 58(1967): 68–72, quoted from 70.

denotes an aspect of the meaning of *monai*. He endorses another aspect which implies the heavenly room literally.[63] Consequently, Gundry emphasizes the double meaning of *monai*. His argument, however, lacks sufficient evidence. The evidences he presents for the second meaning as the literal heavenly room are I Enoch 39.4f; 41.2; 45.3; II Enoch 61.2a; and John 7.34,36; 17.24. Gundry violates the law of assumptions. The fact that I and II Enoch presuppose the literal heavenly location does not necessarily imply that John 14.2 denotes the literal location. His position itself that John 14.2 can be interpreted in terms of double meaning should presuppose that John could enlarge the literal sense of the term appeared in I and II Enoch. Furthermore, several verses in John 7 and 17 he presents denote not the literal sense, but the spiritual sense of the term. For example, Jesus says to the officers of the chief priests and Pharisees: "Where I am you cannot come"(7.34,36). This saying of Jesus implies, contrary to Gundry, not the literal location, but the spiritual sphere. In other words, the saying is to be paraphrased as follows: "You cannot come into the sphere of glory where I am."

This section(14.1-3) reflects the Johannine community's dispute against the apostolic Jewish Christians who hesitate to admit Jesus as God. 14.1 attacks the Jewish proclivity which distinguishes between the belief in God and the belief in Jesus. To believe in God is to believe in Jesus for John. Jesus' preparation of a spiritual place for his followers(14.2), and his permission for them to enter the sphere of glory(14.3) denote that Jesus' power is equal to God. Only God has the authority to do them. Thus, this section rejects the Jewish notion which distinguishes between God and Jesus, rather than the notion which abolishes the distinction between Jesus and his successors.

In 14.4 Jesus says, "you know the way where I am going."

---

63. *Ibid.*, 71.

Thomas, one of Jesus' disciples, responds that "we do not know where you are going; how can we know the way?" (14.5). Why does Thomas express such a response, in spite of Jesus' declaration that "you know"? D. B. Woll eliminates this difficult question in his argument. 14.4 denotes that Jesus is the way to the Father. Jesus declares that "you know the way(=Jesus)" with a presupposition that the way and himself are identical but Thomas responds that they do not know the way since they separate the notion of the way from Jesus. In other words, the disciples know only Jesus separated from the way to God. Jesus claims that "I am the way"(14.6). Thus, verse 5 criticizes not only Thomas but the disciples who do not know this point.

Jesus is shown to be the exclusive mediator to the Father: "I am the way, and the truth, and the life; no one comes to the Father, but by me"(14.6). If the disciples are to reach the Father, they must continue to cling to Jesus, and abide in him through belief in him. What is the social *Sitz im Leben* for this verse or for the first farewell discourse as a whole? Who are the objects of John's attack implied in Jesus' address? O. Cullmann argues that the evangelist attacks the disciples of John the Baptist here.[64] Cullmann's argument is highly questionable, since Jesus' address here is directed to his disciples, and he rejects their views of himself. Unlike Cullmann, F. F. Segovia regards the evangelist's opponents as the Jews.

> The proposed *Sitz im Leben* for this first farewell discourse of
> 13:31–14:31 is very similar indeed to that generally ascribed to
> the Fourth Gospel as a whole by contemporary Johannine
> scholarship, namely, a prolonged and bitter confrontation
> between a Christian community and a parent synagogue(s)
> from which most of the former's present members have been

---

64. O. Cullmann, *The Johannine Circle*(Philadelphia: The Westminster Press, 1976), p.60.

forced to separate because of their belief in Jesus.[65]

Segovia's proposition is less compelling. The Jews of course are one of the objects of John's attack in the Fourth Gospel, especially in chapters 8 and 9. But John's opponents are not depicted as an exclusive color throughout the Gospel. Segovia seems to fail to distinguish between *Sitz im Leben* for the first farewell discourse and *Sitz im Leben* for the Gospel as a whole. The general picture of conflict between the Johannine community and the Jews does not fit to the specific conflict implied in the first farewell discourse. The first farewell discourse, of course, reflects John's criticism against the Jews to a certain degree. But it is marginal, and it does not control the proclivity of the discourse for John applies his criticism against the Jews to the disciples here. F. F. Segovia maintains that the redactor has revised the first farewell discourse in the light of the new situation in the community. According to him, the redactor directs the discourse to argue against the position of the deviant group.[66] This argument is plausible but not demonstrable. According to Segovia, the sharp distinction between the disciples and "the world" in the first farewell discourse is blurred after the redactor's activity. He presupposes that the position of some of the disciples ("deviant group") is identical to that of the Jews.

> In conclusion, for the redactor, the disciples were no longer all the same; in fact, some had joined "the world"(1John 4:1,5).[67]

Segovia identifies the situation of the first farewell discourse revised by the redactor with that of I John. Both situations, however, are not identical to each other, since I John shows explicitly the later period of schism of the Johannine community

---

65. F. F. Segovia, "The Structure," 490.

66. *Ibid.*, 493.

67. *Ibid.*, 493.

(I Jn.2.19), while the Gospel does not exhibit the explicit schism. Moreover, Segovia posits that "some" of the disciples joined the world, but the discourse directs not to "some" of the disciples, but to the whole disciples.

The notion of 14.6 originates from the Johannine community's dispute against the apostolic Jewish Christians who do not recognize that Jesus is the way. They remain in the low christology which regards Jesus as the Christ. They do not accept the high christology. D. B. Woll articulates that 14.6 is "directed against a view which holds that Jesus is *replaced* by successor figures."[68] According to Woll, John rejects those who

> were illegitimately placing themselves on a level with Jesus and were thus setting themselves up as rivals to Jesus. .... The author understands the successor as a subordinate to Jesus.[69]

Woll's argument is creative, but less satisfactory. For what is disputed here is not the charismatic notion of Jesus' successors, but the traditional theo-logy of the apostolic Jewish Christians who distinguish between God and Jesus. The disciples are criticized by Jesus for their distinction between their belief in God and their belief in Jesus(14.1). Jesus' declaration, "no one comes to the Father, but by me," is not presented to distinguish between the Father and Jesus. It advocates the notion that without Jesus there is not the Father, and without Jesus the Father is not to be perceived. Jesus and the Father are one(10.30).

This notion is confirmed by the following section. Jesus' correction of Thomas' position is extended to the disciples ("you"-plural) as a whole: "If you had known me, you would have known my Father also; from now on, you know him and have seen him"(14.7). F. F. Segovia postulates that the failure

---

68. D. B. Woll, *Johannine Christianity in Conflict*, p.66.
69. *Ibid.*, p.66.

of the disciples

is balanced and softened by the declaration of v 7 to the effect that "from now on" the disciples do know and have seen the Father.[70]

Segovia's postulation cannot be sustained, since as verse 8 shows, the failure of the disciples is not "softened" but "strengthened." In other words. if the verse 7 is to be understood in light of verses 8-9, v.7b may be paraphrased as follows: "If you identify me with the Father, from now on you know him and have seen him." However, because they do not identify Jesus with the Father, by implication, they do not know and have not seen not only Jesus but the Father. This is the meaning of v.7a: "If you had known me, you would have known my Father also."

Philip's request to Jesus' address displays that he does not retain the high christology which identifies Jesus as the Father. Philip is severely criticized by Jesus here. Jesus has been with Philip for "so long," but the latter does not know the former. Jesus' criticism against Philip is extended to the whole disciples("you"-plural) in v.9. Jesus has spent "so long" a time not only with Philip but with the disciples. Why does John emphasize this long period of disciples' fellowship with Jesus? The present authority of the apostolic Jewish Christians is dependent on the lengthy period of fellowship the past disciples enjoyed with Jesus. John questions the period itself. Despite their lengthy period of fellowship with Jesus, the disciples did not recognize the fact that the one who has seen him has seen the Father. The author weakens the foundation on which the authority of the apostolic Jewish Christians is dependent.

The author rejects the apostolic Jewish Christians who do

---

70. F. F. Segovia, "The Structure," 483f.

not believe in the oneness between Jesus and God(14.9), and in the reciprocal abodes between them(14.10). The Johannine Jesus demands again for those Christians to believe it: "Believe me that I am in the Father and the Father in me; or else believe me for the sake of the works themselves"(14.11). Jesus criticizes the disciples who, in a long period, have seen the "works" Jesus performed, but have not perceived the oneness between himself and God. This is the reason why the name of Jesus is emphasized again(14.13,14,26). The author is aware that Jesus has been absorbed in the traditional theo-logy of the apostolic Jewish Christians.

In 14.13 the Johannine Jesus announces that "whatever you ask in my name, I will do it, that the Father may be glorified in the Son." This announcement reflects on the practice of the apostolic Jewish Christians, that their activities are performed without Jesus' name. They cannot glorify the Father, unless they keep the name of Jesus in their minds. The Father may be glorified in(*en*) the Son. Without the Son, the Father may not be glorified. The Son glorified the Father on earth(17.4).

The conflict between the Johannine community and the apostolic Jewish Christians is also reflected in 14.16-17. What is the relationship between Jesus and another Paraclete in this passage? G. Bornkamm posits that in the tradition, Jesus as a forerunner was subordinated to the Paraclete as a fulfiller,[71] but modifying the tradition, John not only has reversed the hierarchical order between Jesus and the Paraclete,[72] but has made the two distinct figures be one and the same.[73] D. B. Woll's criticism against Bornkamm is very convincing. According to Woll, Bornkamm's presupposition that the first of the two figures is inferior to the second cannot be sustained,

---

71. G. Bornkamm, "Der Paraklet im Johannes Evangelium," in *Geschichte und Glaube*, Part I , Collected Essays, vol.3(München: Chr. Kaiser Verlag, 1968), p.71.

72. *Ibid.*, p.87.

73. *Ibid.*, p.79.

as the example of Moses and Joshua, or Elijah and Elisha demonstrates.[74] Woll maintains, unlike Bornkamm, that John accepts his opponents' premise that priority means superiority, but he applies it "in a radical way." For John, the time of the Paraclete is subordinated to the prior time of Jesus.[75]

Despite the differences between Bornkamm and Woll, both scholars agree with each other in the sense that the Paraclete passage presupposes the order of time. The passage, however, is introduced not to emphasize the temporal differences between Jesus and the Paraclete, but to set forth John's dispute against his competing group's understanding of the Paraclete. What is the relationship of Jesus to the "other" Paraclete? O. Betz proposes that the archangel Michael was the prototype for the two distinct figures in John. Michael played dual roles in heaven and on earth respectively. For John these dual roles are assigned to the exalted Christ in heaven, and to the Paraclete on earth.[76] This proposition is quite doubtful, since the roles of Jesus and the Paraclete are identical in many respects as 14.17,26 attest. Moreover Betz does not secure any foundations to support his proposition in the text itself of John's Gospel.

U. B. Müller presupposes that the notion in which the Spirit on earth represents the heavenly Christ was circulated in John's contemporary. According to him, John related the Spirit to the Christ more closely, and integrated them to be one and the same.[77] Müller's position is less satisfactory, since he does not solve the problem of why John retains "another" just before "Paraclete," even after his integration of the two figures into one and the same. H. Windisch tries to explain the relationship between Jesus and the "another" Paraclete in

---

74. D. B. Woll, *Johannine Christianity in Conflict*, p.76.

75. *Ibid.*, p.77.

76. O. Betz, *Der Paraklet*(Leiden: E. J. Brill, 1963), p.149f.

77. U. B. Müller, "Die Parakletenvorstellung in Johannesevangelium," *ZTK* 71(1974): 45f.

terms of the difference between the traditional strata.[78] His explanation, however, remains unproved. For if the difference is resulted from the different strata, the final redactor of the Gospel would modify some aspects of the strata.

The world knows neither Jesus nor the Paraclete. Not only Jesus but the Paraclete dwells in the disciples. The Paraclete presents nothing more than Jesus. The Paraclete takes over the teaching activity of Jesus(14.26a), and makes the disciples remember it(14.26b). John presents Jesus as the truth(14.6). The Paraclete is portrayed as the Spirit of truth(14.17). Consequently, it is natural to assume that the Paraclete is another name of Jesus. Then, why does John retain the title, the "another" Paraclete? John uses it partly to admit the position of the apostolic Jewish Christians, and at the same time to criticize it. They claimed that they were with the another Paraclete who is different from the earthly Jesus. John admits their term, another Paraclete, and persuades them to perceive that another Paraclete and Jesus are the same figure. This is the reason why the activity of the earthly Jesus is not suspended despite his departure. He lives(19b). Jesus continues his work in the form of the Paraclete even after his death. This is the meaning of 14.19: "After a little while the world will see me no longer, but you will see me; because I live, you will live too." Jesus says to the disciples that they will see him in another form even after his death. The another Paraclete "must mean that Jesus is describing himself indirectly as the Paraclete."[79] Jesus and the Paraclete are different in the sense that their modes of presence are not identical.[80] The apostolic Jewish Christians confused the

---

78. H. Windisch, *The Spirit Paraclete in the Fourth Gospel* (Philadelphia: Fortress Press, 1968), p.25.

79. R. Schnackenburg, *John*, III, p.74.

80. E. Malatesta explores that the mission of the Paraclete is both similar and distinct from the mission of Jesus. "The Spirit/Paraclete in the Fourth Gospel," *Biblica* 54(1973): 539–550, esp. 549.

difference of presence modes with the difference of being. When Jesus' earthly mode of presence, which includes spirit and flesh, is changed into the different mode of presence which includes spirit only, the glory of Jesus is restored.

The disciples are anticipated to meet a difficult situation after Jesus' death. Jesus promises that he will not leave them desolate, and he is coming(*erkhomai*) to them(14.18). Jesus "is coming" to them after his departure. This promise reflects a situation that the apostolic Jewish Christians do not recognize the presence of Jesus in the form of the Paraclete. They do not perceive the Paraclete, who is presently with them, as Jesus. They misunderstand the Paraclete as the "another" one who is different from Jesus. Thus, verse 14.18 functions as criticism against the apostolic Jewish Christians who do not perceive the presence of Jesus who "lives"(14.19). Furthermore, they are desolated, since they do not recognize that Jesus as the Paraclete who "is coming"(*erkhomai*) to them.

The Paraclete will glorify Jesus, for he will take what is Jesus' and declare it to the disciples(16.14). The Paraclete will not speak on his own authority, but whatever he hears he will speak(16.13). Here the Paraclete does nothing more than Jesus. He will guide the disciples into all "the truth"(16.13). J. A. Draper notes that

> the concept of 'truth' relates to boundary maintenance between members and non-members of the community.... The Paraclete sayings serve to cut off the community member from the outside world, by giving society beyond the sect a negative valuation as the sphere of the operation of demonic forces. This, in turn, is linked with the strongest possible valuation of inner group interaction or love.[81]

---

81. J. A. Draper,"The Sociological Function of the Spirit/Paraclete in the Farewell Discourses in the Fourth Gospel," *Neotestamentica* 26(1, 1992): 13-29, quoted from 26-27.

Draper's general information seems to be valid, but he does not inform us of the peculiar features of the Johannine community and its competing group. The Johannine community members regard themselves as those who correctly understand the Jesus tradition more so than the apostolic Jewish Christians, and those who are real successors, namely, real disciples of Jesus. For Jesus himself announces that "I am not speaking of you all; I know whom I have chosen" (13.18).[82] The community members draw boundary lines not only between the Jews and themselves, but the apostolic Jewish Christians and themselves as well. In this sense, they are characterized as a sectarian group.[83]

The countergroup to which the Johannine community opposes or competes against is the apostolic Jewish Christians outside the community. In this sense I do not agree with D. B. Woll's hypothesis that the counter-group is rather the "charismatic claimants" within the Johannine community. Woll argues that there are two kinds of charismatic groups within the Johannine community: One group emphasizes its direct access to the ultimate power, while the other group stresses its mediated authority.[84] According to Woll, John, who is a representative of the latter group, tries to correct the position of the former group.

Woll's solution meets two difficult problems. First, his proposed charismatic situation of the Johannine community

---

82. For the informative study on 13.18, see M. J. J. Menken, "The Translation of Psalm 41.10 in John 13.18," *JSNT* 40(1990): 61-79. Menken concludes that "John could not use the LXX translation of Ps.41(40).10, because it was at variance with his ideas about Jesus' omniscience." John uses his own translation.

83. John Painter proposes that John uses a 'sectarian' Jewish hymn as the basis of his prologue. "Christology and the History of the Johannine Community in the Prologue of the Fourth Gospel," *NTS* 30(1984): 460-474.

84. D. B. Woll, *The Johannine Christianity in Conflict*, p.127f.

does not fit with the desolate situation implied in 14.18. The charismatic workers regard themselves as the chosen. Superiority rather than inferiority, and the sense of confidence rather than the sense of shrinking typify them. Woll does not concentrate on 14.18, since it may weaken his characterization of the community with charismatic proclivity. Second, Woll sees John belonging to the charismatic group which emphasizes on "mediation" or "hierarchical order." According to Woll,

> the author and those he is countering were very likely drawing on the same charismatic tradition of origin.[85]

Woll characterizes the author's group as less charismatic than its counterpart. This argument is highly questionable. A group which stresses mediation or hierarchical order is no longer charismatic in a strict sense. Rather, it is against the charismatic proclivity. Thus, John's group, contrary to Woll, cannot belong to "the same charismatic tradition."

The Johannine community's criticism against the apostolic Jewish Christians is also disclosed in 14.23: "If anyone loves me... my Father will love him/her, and we will come to him/her and make our home with him/her." Here Jesus and the Father are introduced with the expression "we." It is directed to repute against the apostolic Jewish Christians who separate Jesus from God. Jesus, of course, is less than the Father(14.28) before his entering into the sphere of glory, but Jesus is identical to the Father after his restoration of the former glory which he had with the Father "before the world was made"(17.5).

In 14.27 Jesus announces that he leaves peace with the disciples. His peace is characterized "not as the world gives." His admonition continues: "Let not your hearts be troubled,

---

85. *Ibid.*, p.128.

neither let them be afraid." The "world" here denotes the Jews. Peace of the world is contrasted with peace of Jesus. P. S. Minear's note on this is illuminating.

> The opposite of peace is defined in a double way. It is set over against the world's peace and against hearts controlled by fear. Both thoughts are essential.... It [world's peace] is peace readily available to believers who keep their faith hidden, or who, like Judas, become informer, or who, like Peter, deny any knowledge of Jesus. .... "Don't be frightened by the authority and power of your adversaries. Don't try to buy security by betraying me. Don't let your fear of death prompt compromises with my enemies..."[86]

The thought in 14.27 demonstrates that if there are those who are frightened, it is because they lack Jesus' peace. Jesus' announcement in 14.27 reflects that there is the absence of Jesus' peace in the apostolic Jewish Christians. They are satisfied with the world's peace and consequently, their minds, in the author's eyes, are frightened and troubled. Contrasting the peace of his community, namely, the peace of Jesus with the peace of the apostolic Jewish Christians, namely, the peace of the world, John disputes against them efficiently.

The Johannine Jesus speaks of analogy of the vine and the branches in 15.1-6. He emphasizes that apart from him, they can do nothing(15.5). Those who do not abide in him are cast forth as a branch and withers(15.6). The abiding means remaining in fellowship with Jesus. As Joseph C. Dillow notes, "the analogy of the vine and the branches signifies not organic connection with Christ but fellowship with Him."[87] In John's eyes the apostolic Jewish Christians do not abide in

---

86. P. S. Minear, *John. The Martyr's Gospel*, p.60.

87. J. C. Dillow, "Abiding Is Remaining in Fellowship: Another Look at John 15:1-6," *Bib Sacra* 147(1990): 44-53, esp. 53.

Jesus, and thus do not remain in fellowship with him.

The ideal past representatives of the apostolic Jewish Christians are to be sought not only in Peter, Philip, Thomas, Judas and other disciples but in Nicodemus. According to Michael Goulder, John views Nicodemus

> as a representative of Jewish Christianity, that is, the Jerusalem Christianity led by James and Peter, that was in competition with the Pauline mission. .... Nicodemus is a Jewish Christian, ... Jewish Christians are subsumed with 'the Jews.' [88]

I agree with him that Nicodemus is a representative of Jewish Christianity, but I do not agree with him in the sense that Jewish Christianity is not to be easily identified with the Jerusalem Christianity led by James and Peter. For "Jewish Christianity" is an umbrella concept which embraces so many similar groups. James as the brother of Jesus, who was a prominent figure in the Pauline epistles (Gal. 1.19; 2.9, 12; I Cor. 15.7), never appears in the Gospel of John. Thus, the apostolic Jewish Christianity, as the countergroup of the Johannine community, seems to be a group which was originated and separated from the Jerusalem Jewish Christianity. The apostolic Jewish Christians seem to disregard James as the brother of Jesus, and to find their past ideal figure not in James but in Peter.

Since the glory is an interrelational term which requires recognition of one party toward another, the glory of the Johannine community is acquired when people recognize that the community members' understanding of Jesus and of themselves are supreme over against those of others.

---

88. M. Goulder, "Nicodemus," *SJT* 44(2, 1992): 153-168, quoted from 153, 168.

CHAPTER III

RESTORATION OF GLORY

CHAPTER III
RESTORATION OF GLORY

1. Jesus' Restoration of Glory

The Johannine Jesus is called the "Son of God"(*ho hyios tou theou*). Sometimes Jesus used the title for himself. John introduces this title to emphasize Jesus' divine origin, but he proceeds further. He claims that Jesus is God. What is the social context for those designations of the "Son of God" and "God" and what is the relationship between the theme of glory and those designations?

Jesus as the Son of God

The Son of God is one of the most prominent designations for Jesus in the Fourth Gospel. John the Baptist testifies that Jesus is the Son of God(1.34). Nathanael recognizes Jesus as the Son of God(1.49). Attacked by the Jews, Jesus boldly declares that "I am God's Son"(10.36). The accusation of the Jews to Pilate was that "Jesus claimed to be the Son of God" (19.7). Jesus is introduced as the "one and only"(*monogenous*) Son(3.18). Not only do the believers in the Son receive eternal life, even the dead "now" hear his voice(5.24f.). The cause of Nazarus' illness was understood in the light of God's glory which will be received by the "Son of God," and of Jesus' glory which will be received by means of it(11.3-4). Also, Martha, the sister of Nazarus, professes to believe Jesus as the Son of God(11.27). The purpose of the Gospel, stated in the concluding verses(20.30-31) is to make clear to believe that "Jesus is the Son of God."

Jesus is often called a prophet (4.19;6.14), but as Adele Reinhartz argues convincingly, "Jesus is not only a forthteller, but a foreteller as well."[1] John demonstrates Jesus' ability to proclaim future events. According to Reinhartz,

> the main purpose of this device [prediction and occurrence] is not, however, to indicate Jesus' place among the prophets but to point to his unique identity as the Son of God, who has been given the authority to speak God's words and to do God's works in the world.[2]

John differs from other evangelists in his uses of the christological titles. Not only the title 'prophet', but the titles 'son of God' and 'son of Man' "are given a new depth by John," who sets the titles in the background against "his understanding of the 'pre-existence' of the Revealer."[3]

The title, "Son of God" is utilized to emphasize Jesus' divine origin and his divine presence. The one and only Son of God promises to give breath to those that are dead and eternal life to those who believe. The works, once attributed to the Father, the Son accomplishes. Jesus, as the Son of God prays thus:

> "For you(Father) granted him(Son) authority over all people that he might give eternal life to those you have given him." (17.2).

All that the Son has belongs to the Father and all that the Father has is the Son's(17.10). Viewed from the position of the Son, the entrusting of the Father's authority to the Son

---

1. A. Reinhartz "Jesus as Prophet: Predictive Prolepses in the Fourth Gospel," *JSNT* 36(1989): 3-16, quoted from 12.

2. *Ibid.*, 12.

3. J. Painter, "Christology and the Fourth Gospel. A Study of the Prologue," *ABR* 31(1983): 45-62, quoted from 45.

becomes the glory of the Son, but it is stated clearly that the Son is glorified by the Father with the intent that the Father might be glorified(17.1).

Jesus does not glorify himself. He does not seek his own glory but the glory of the Father(7.18). Furthermore, he rejects the glorification that originates from men: "I do not accept praise from human beings"(*para anthrōpōn*)(5.14), but rather, he criticizes the Jews for not seeking "the praise that comes from the only God"(*para tou theou*)(5.44c). Even when he entreats the Father to glorify him, he reveals his purpose, that he may glorify the Father(17.1). These statements were aimed at the Jews who sought only after the praises(glory) "from one another"(*para allēlōn*) rather than praises(glory) that comes from God(5.44b). "For they loved praise from human beings more than praise from God"(12.43). Unlike the Jews who did not realize that the true glory came from God, Jesus understood the glory in relation to God.

The title, the "Son of God" denotes Jesus' status on earth. He was sent by God. He is the ambassador of God. When he was with God in heaven, he was equal to Him. But Jesus forfeited his equality to God when he was sent by Him and descended from heaven. Jesus' mission on earth is to make the people believe in him who is the Son of God, and have eternal life(3.16; 20.31). Thus, Jesus' mission and his status as the Son of God is closely interrelated in John's Gospel. John Ashton presents this very clearly in his careful discussion of Jesus' relationship with God.

> Essentially John saw Jesus' relationship with God in two clearly distinguishable ways, *sonship*, and *mission*... In chapter 7 the term 'Father' is not used: nowhere in this chapter is there the slightest hint that Jesus regarded himself as the Son of God.[4]

---

4. John Ashton, *Understanding the Fourth Gospel*(Oxford: Clarendon Press, 1991), p.318.

According to Ashton, the idea of sonship and the idea of mission, both of which were originally separated from each other, are fused together in John's Gospel.

> The most valuable result has been the discovery of a thought-world that makes sense of the evangelist's picture of Jesus as the Son of God entrusted by him with a message for the world.[5]

The disciples' report about a group of Greeks who wish to see Jesus(12.20) is followed by Jesus' answer: "The hour has come for the Son of Man to be glorified"(12.23). This incident means that the mission of Jesus as God's emissary is being accomplished. Jesus proceeds further to ask the Father to glorify His name(12.28). The glory of the Father comes from the completion of Jesus' mission. The indirect coming of the Greeks to Jesus is a sign of hour of Jesus' death in terms of departure. This is the reason why Jesus' answer is followed by the explanation about the death of the grain of wheat falling onto the earth.

According to the evangelist, although Jesus forfeits his equality to God on earth, he retains his divinity in the fleshy life as the Son of God(1.14; 2.11). W. R. G. Loader fails to distinguish between Jesus' glory as God and his glory as the Son of God when he argues as follows.

> ... in the cluster Jesus' glorification is his return to that glory (12.23; 13.31; 7.39,12,16; cf.17.5). In the structure, however, there is emphasis on Jesus' glory being seen already on earth (1.14,18; 2.11; 11.4). The two ideas are in tension.[6]

In John, Jesus only forfeits his equality to God when he was

---

5. *Ibid.*, p.328.
6. W. R. G. Loader, "The Central Structure of Johannine Christology," *NTS* 30(1984): 188-216, quoted from 201.

sent by Him. Despite his descent onto earth Jesus retains his "divinity as the Son of God" in his flesh. In this sense, John differs from Paul who asserts Jesus' emptiness on earth(Phil.2.7). The glory of Jesus is partly restored when the people recognize him as God's Son sent by Him. John confines those people as those whom the Father gave Jesus out of the world(17.6), since it is impossible that all the people on earth recognize Jesus as God's Son. They know now that Jesus came from God, and they believe that God did send him(17.8), and that he is God's Son(3.16). Jesus begins to restore his glory because the chosen people recognize his status as the Son of God on earth and his mission for believing in him and having the eternal life. This is the initial restoration of Jesus' glory.

Jesus as God

John the author does not limit his story to describing Jesus' divine origin and his divinity in the flesh. In the final analysis, the Gospel of John presents Jesus as God. This is most clearly emphasized in the prologue of John's Gospel where Logos christology is revealed. As David L. Mealand notes, "though Jesus is rarely called God in the New Testament, this does occur, probably in passing, in the Pastoral Epistles, and with deliberate emphasis"[7] in John. In the prologue the Word become flesh(1.14) is proclaimed as "God"(1.1). Of course, the relationship between the prologue of the Gospel of John to the rest of the Gospel has been problematic. The problem has been researched from many different angles, but because the discussion of this topic goes beyond the scope of this paper, it will not be further inquired. It is sufficient to state that although some of the terminologies

---

7. D. L. Mealand, "The Christology of the Fourth Gospel," *SJT* 31(1978): 449-467, quoted from 463.

found in the prologue does not appear anywhere else in the Gospel, or conversely, certain style(language) in the body of the Gospel does not appear in the prologue, the idea present in the prologue and the idea present in the rest of the Gospel concur, at the least, in the similarity of thought and color.

John uses the title "the Savior of the world" for Jesus to denote Jesus' equality to God. The Samaritans acclaim Jesus as "the Savior of the world"(4.42). This title along with "God" culminates a series of affirmations of Jesus' divinity. C. R. Koester explores the similarity between the imperial use of the title and John 4.42.[8] Although he inclines to argue that the title was used for the emperor, Koester acknowledges its wide currency in the Greco-Roman world.

> The title "savior" itself was used in various ways in the ancient world and was not reserved for imperial use. In Greco-Roman sources it was used for gods like Zeus, Asclepius, Isis, and Serapis, and for philosophers and leaders of various ranks. The translators of the LXX also used the title both for God(e.g., Isa 45:15, 21) and for human delievers like Othniel and Ehud(Judg 3:9, 15). Philo occasionally called God "savior of the world"... and "savior of all"... and in the second century the orator Aelius Aristides referred to the god Asclepius as "savior of all people"... and "savior of all."[9]

With this title "the Savior of the world," John tries to demonstrate that it was, as Richard J. Cassidy articulates, "Jesus and not Nero or any other emperor who was truly *Savior of the world.* It was, of course, Jesus and not Domitian or any other emperor who was truly *Lord and God.* No Roman emperor of any age, but only Jesus shows the way to the Father and the life that is everlasting."[10] John uses this

---

8. C. R. Koester, "The Savior of the World(John 4:42)," *JBL* 109 (4, 1990): 665-680.

9. *Ibid.,* 666.

10. Richard J. Cassidy, *John's Gospel in New Perspective*

title "the Savior of the world" nowhere else in his Gospel.
Unlike the usage in Judges 3, John uses the title for Jesus in
light of Isaiah 45. In Judges 3 the political leaders are called
the savior, while in Isaiah 45 God is the Savior. In John
4.42 there is no political implication in the portrayal of Jesus.
John uses the title here in order to denote Jesus' equality to
God.

John presents Jesus' equality to God in a peculiar form.
Jesus' statements, "If you had known me, you would have
known my Father also,"(14.7) and "One who has seen me has
seen the Father"(14.9) reveals his equality to God. Jesus and
the Father are expressed by "we"(14.23; 17.11,22,23). Jesus
claims that he and the Father are one(10.30). If A is equal to
B, A must include B and at the same time B must include A.
The reciprocal inclusiveness is the primary condition to
equality. John presents that Jesus is in the Father, and the
Father is in him(14.20; 17.21). John confesses Jesus as God
through the mouth of Thomas in the concluding remarks of
his Gospel(20.28). I John confirms this idea in a dogmatic
formula: "This [Jesus] is the true God and eternal life"(I
Jn.5.20).

John presents mutual glorification between Jesus and God.
In 13.31 Jesus is glorified(*edoxasthē*), and in him God is
glorified(*edoxasthē*). G. B. Caird rejects the idea of this mutual
glorification in his exegesis on 13.31.[11] According to him, the
first "*edoxasthē*" can be translated as true passive, while the
second "*edoxasthē*" cannot be translated as true passive.

There are many passive forms which are not true passives...
There are deponents of which on active form exists. But there

---

Christology and the Realities of Roman Power(Maryknoll, New York:
Orbis Books, 1992), p.55.

11. G. B. Caird, "The Glory of God in the Fourth Gospel: An
Exercise in Biblical Semantics," *NTS*(1969): 265-277.

are also many verbs in which both active and passive indicate action done by the subject, the difference being that the one is transitive and the other intransitive... Moreover, it frequently happens that the same passive form can be used either as a true passive or as an intransitive.[12]

In Caird's assertion, the second *"edoxasthē"* is to be perceived as intransitive passive which denotes active. He paraphrases 13.31 as the following: "Now the Son of Man has been endowed with glory, and God has revealed his glory in him."[13]

Caird's note that a passive form denotes an active meaning in Greek is of course true. But it does not necessarily imply that the second *"edoxasthē"* in 13.31 is to be regarded as the intransitive. For, if John wished to distinguish the contents of the first word and the second word, he would replace the second word with *"edoxade."* Thus, against Caird, it is a natural conclusion that both the first word and the second word in 13.31 are used in the same usage. The reason why Caird concentrates on this verse lies in his theological presupposition that God's glory comes solely from Himself, not from anyone including Jesus. This presupposition, however, does not fit into the theology of John. The evangelist elsewhere already uncovers that Jesus glorifies God(17.4; 17.1,5).

In many instances, John presents the reciprocal glorification between Jesus and God. This reciprocal glorification becomes another ground for the oneness between Jesus and God. This reciprocity reflects a social context in which the Johannine community criticizes against those who separate Jesus from God with the purpose being to believe only in God. John emphasizes a close interrelationship between the glory of God and the glory of Jesus.

---

12. *Ibid.*, 268.
13. *Ibid.*, 271.

If Jesus and God are one and the same, why does the Johannine Jesus state that "the Father is greater than I" (14.28)? J. Ashton brings this paradox out very clearly and tries to solve the problem.

> This contradiction can only be resolved by bearing in mind that Jesus' relationship with God continues throughout to be conceived on the analogy of the prophetic mission and the law of agency. The paradox of the parity between the sender and the sent cannot be maintained at its proper point of equilibrium unless both its terms are kept in sight. *In fact* the king is greater than his emissary; *in law* the emissary is the king's equal.[14)]

Ashton's solution is less than satisfactory. I suspect that the reverse is true. Rather, "in fact," contrary to Ashton, Jesus is equal to God. But when Jesus is sent by God and is descended from heaven, he becomes less than God. When he departs earth and ascends to heaven, he restores his glory that he had with God(17.5), that is, he regains his equality to God. Thus, the Johannine Jesus could state his subordination to God in reflection of his earthly life on one hand, and his equality to God either retrospectively or prospectively on the other hand.

The full restoration of Jesus' glory is accomplished when the people whom the Father gave him "out of the world"(17.6) recognize Jesus' regaining of his equality to God after his ascension to heaven. Jesus, as W. H. Kelber notes, seems to incarnate himself "in order to bring about a return to origin."[15)] The Johannine Jesus entreats that the people whom the Father has given him may be with him where he is, so they

---

14. J. Ashton, *Understanding the Fourth Gospel*, p.316.

15. W. H. Kelber, "In the Beginning were the Words. The Apotheosis and Narrative Displacement of the Logos," *JAAR* 58(1, 1990): 69–98, esp.93.

may behold his glory which the Father has given him in His love for him before the foundation of the world(17.24). In John Jesus is regarded as "God" who was in the bosom of the Father(1.18). The Logos was God(1.1).

The statements in regard to the mutual abiding between Jesus and God reflect the Johannine community's criticism against those who separate Jesus from God. One of its antagonists' propositions was "Jesus and the Father are not the same"(cf.10.30). In their theology, the reciprocal inclusiveness between Jesus and God was quite doubtful. The Father's is the Father's, and Jesus' is Jesus' for them(cf.17.10). They assert that the eternal life comes from knowing of the only true God without knowing of Jesus(cf. 17.3). The Johannine community reputes againt this assertion. To know and believe in Jesus is to know and believe in God(14.7). To have the eternal life in Jesus is to have it in God(17.3). B. A. Mastin maintains that

> ... it is reasonable to claim that the Evangelist thought it was important that the title *theos* should be given to Jesus. It is probable that this feature of his christology is due to controversy with the Jews, and that as a result of this he formulated his estimate of Christ's person in this way.[16]

G. Reim endorses Mastin's argument and presents the scriptural background for it.[17] But the title *theos* given to Jesus in the Gospel does not necessarily reflect the controversy with the Jews exclusively. Rather, it reflects the controversies not only with the Jews, but with the apostolic Jewish Christians who separate Jesus from God. J. H. Neyrey proposes that Jesus is properly called "equal to God,"

---

16. B. A. Mastin, "A Neglected Feature of the Christology of the Fourth Gospel," *NTS* 22(1975): 32-51, quoted from 51.

17. G. Reim, "Jesus as God in the Fourth Gospel: The Old Testament Background," *NTS* 30(1984): 158-160.

because he has God's two basic power(creative/eschatological).

> Creative power is not only claimed but demonstrated (1:1-18;
> 5:1-9,19-20) and so Jesus is rightly called Theos. Eschatological
> power is initially only claimed in 5:18,21-29, and its demonstration
> remains the task of the rest of the gospel.[18]

Neyrey's proposition is convincing, but he misses another important point of Jesus' presence itself: Jesus is called God in the sense that Jesus is with God before the foundation of the world. In heaven, Jesus, before or after the earthly life, is equal to God. The prerequisite to the full restoration of the forfeited glory of Jesus is his departing the earth for heaven.

2. The Community's Restoration of Glory

W. R. Cook asserts that "the glory of God is central to Johannine thought."[19] Cook is only partially correct, because he misses the point that the glory of the Johannine community is at least as central to the Gospel. At best, the glory of the Johannine community is more important than the glory of God in that the characteristics of the former determine the color of the latter.

Believers as children of God

One of the major self-definitions of the Johannine community members is "children of God"(*tekna theou*). This

---

18. J. H. Neyrey, "'My Lord and My God': The Divinity of Jesus in John's Gospel," in *SBL Seminar Papers* (Atlanta, Georgia: Scholars Press, 1988), pp.152-171, quoted from p.158.

19. W. R. Cook, "The 'Glory' Motif in the Johannine Corpus," 297.

self-definition appears in 1.12 and 11.52. Especially in the prologue of John's Gospel the "children of God" is a decisive concept for those who claim to have divinity in themselves. Although the title is immediately followed by the phrase "who were born... out of God(*ek theou*)," the latter is merely a modifier to explain it. John places the title in the pivot(1.10c-13) of the prologue of John's Gospel.

R. E. Brown maintains that verses 11 and 12 of the prologue epitomize the two major parts of the Gospel respectively.

> Verses 11 and 12 seem to be a summary of the two main divisions of John. Verse 11 covers the Book of Signs(chs. i - xii), which tells how Jesus came to his own land through a ministry in Galilee and Jerusalem and yet his own people did not receive him. Verse 12 covers the Book of Glory(chs. xiii-xx), which contains Jesus' words to those who did receive him and tells how he returned to his Father in order to give them the gift of life and make them God's children.[20]

Brown's analysis is possible, but not demonstrable. He views the theme of the Book of Signs as the people's "rejection" of Jesus, and the theme of the Book of Glory as the believers' acceptance of him. This attempt, however, simplifies the content of the Gospel in excess. Indeed, the "rejection" theme is introduced even in the Book of Glory, while the "acceptance" theme even in the Book of Signs. In other words, both verses(1.11-12) contain both themes respectively. Thus, it is natural to presuppose that verses 11-12 as a whole summarize the content of the entire Gospel. The title "children of God" is a pivotal phrase in verses 11-12.

The title "children of God" does not appear in the Hebrew Bible or Qumran documents. Among the canonical gospels the title appears only in the Gospel of John. With this title, the

---

20. R. E. Brown, *John*, I , p.19.

Johannine community members define themselves as those who have divinity in their earthly life. They regard themselves as those who were born "from above"(3.3) and "from God"(1.13). Unlike the Jews, the believers are born of water and spirit(3.5). The community members thought they superceded the Jewish blood boundary and their human standards.

How do they become children of God? John asserts that they were born, "not from bloods... but from God"(1.13). As Jesus came forth "from God"(*ek tou theou*; 8.42), so the community members came "from God"(*ek theou*; 1.13).[21] Through the expression "from God," John insinuates that the divine origin of Jesus concurs with the divine origin of the Johannine community. The community members regard themselves as those who retain the divinity in their humanity. They claim that their community is the divine community since they are children of God.

The Johannine Jesus instructs Mary Magdalene to inform his "brothers"(*adelphous*) of his ascending: " I am ascending to my Father and your Father"(20.17). The Father of Jesus is identified with the Father of his brothers here. Jesus and his believing brothers belong to the same status. Furthermore, the believer is defined as friend(*philos*) of Jesus(15.14,15). The term "friend" denotes a peculiar human relationship which is produced by the human beings who belong to the same sphere. As Jesus has divinity, so his friends have it. R. A. Culpepper identifies the title "children of God" with the term "brothers," but he dissociates the term "friend" from the designations of "children of God" and "brothers."

> The term 'friend' ..., however, is used here [15.15] where we might have expected *tekna theou* or *adelphous mou*. The

---

21. The similar expression is also found in chapter 17. As Jesus came from God(*para sou*; 17.8), so they came from God(*para sou*; 17.7).

reason for the substitution seems to be that the change in the status of the disciples was not yet complete because the work of Jesus had not yet been completed. It is only after the resurrection that the disciples are called adelphous mou(my brothers; 20.17).[22]

Culpepper's argument cannot be sustained. Of course, the believers are called Jesus' "brothers" after his resurrection, but John, contrary to Culpepper, regards the believer as Jesus' brothers even "before" his resurrection.

When Jesus saw his mother, and the disciple whom he loved standing near, he said to his mother, "Woman, behold, your son!" Then he said to the disciple, "Behold, your mother!" (19.26-27).

The term *"adelphous"* is omitted here, not because it is the period before Jesus' resurrection, but because the brotherhood between Jesus and the disciple is naturally presupposed. Furthermore, the reason that Jesus calls his followers as "friends" cannot be explained by the presupposition that it is the period before Jesus' resurrection. Rather, the reason is that Jesus has made known to his followers all that he has heard from the Father(15.15). In other words, the believers are called "friends" of Jesus, since they share with Jesus the privilege in knowing the divine secret. Thus, Jesus' "brothers" and "friends" are other names for "children of God." The Johannine community members as children of God acquire the glory to become Jesus' brothers and friends.

The prerequisite to becoming children of God is to believe in the name of Jesus(1.12). The unbelieving Jews cannot become children of God. Of course John does not confine the qualification of children of God to the present members of the Johannine community. Rather, he calls those, who will join the community as the children of God.

---

22. R. A. Culpepper, "The Pivot of John's Prologue," 29.

> He prophesied that Jesus should die for the nation, and not for
> the nation only, but to gather into one the children of God
> (*tekna tou theou*) who are scattered abroad(11.51-52).

J. L. Martyn argues that the expression "children of God"
here denotes the Jewish people.[23] His argument is less than
satisfactory, for the children of God in John is not dependent
on racial bloods but on belief in Jesus. The Johannine
community desires to unite the scattered abroad into it. The
unification task initiated by Jesus has been preserved and
continued by the Johannine community.

The community members' glory are restored through Jesus.
They cannot acquire their glory to become children of God
without Jesus' permission for them. R. Schnackenburg brings
this point out very clearly.

> In fact, *eksousian* could have been omitted..., because in John
> *didonai* alone(with infinitive) can indicate God's bestowal of
> grace...; but it can also be added as a mark of emphasis...
> to lay stress on the power conferred by God.[24]

The people have to believe in the name of Jesus in order to
become children of God. The community members' honor in
becoming Jesus' friends is dependent on his allowance: "No
longer do I call you servants... but I have called you friends"
(15.15). The community's glory in becoming Jesus' brothers
is also dependent on his pronouncements(19.26-27; 20.17).
Thus, the community's acquirement of glory is possible only
through Jesus' initiative and mediation.

Believers as gods

The Johannine community members as children of God who

---

23. J. L. Martyn, *The Gospel of John in Christian History*, p.118.
24. R. Schnackenburg, *John*, I, p.262.

were born from God claim not only to have divine features in themselves, but to be "gods"(*theoi*). John 10.34-36 supports insinuately for this.

> Jesus answered them, "Is it not written in your law, 'I said, you are gods'? If he called them gods to whom the word of God came(and scripture cannot be broken)... (10.34-35)."

This passage of course is introduced to show Jesus' dispute against the Jewish charge, but it also discloses another aspect of self-understanding of the Johannine community. As J. H. Neyrey notes, "the emphasis in John 10.35 is not on Jesus..., but on 'those to whom the word of God came,' who are called 'gods.'"[25] The pronouncement, "I said, you are gods" is a quotation of Psalm 82.6. J. H. Neyrey's thesis on this pronouncement is peculiar. According to him, John understands Psalm 82 in the way it was understood in the Jewish midrash. In the midrashic understanding Israel is called god because of holiness which resulted in deathlessness.[26] According to Neyrey, John 10.34-36 does not explicitly link godlikeness with deathlessness, but only with holiness.[27] In this sense Neyrey suggests that John did not employ "the full midrashic understanding of Psalm 82 which was available to him."[28]

Although Neyrey finds the difference between the midrashic understanding of Psalm 82 and John's understanding of it, he articulates his conclusion as follows.

> Although the midrashim... were written considerably later than the Fourth Gospel, the understanding of Ps 82:6 in John 10:34-36 belongs in that same trajectory of interpretation.[29]

---

25. J. H. Neyrey, "'I said: You are gods': Psalm 82:6 and John 10," *JBL* 108(1989): 647-663, quoted from 655.

26. *Ibid.*, 656f.

27. *Ibid.*, 659.

28. *Ibid.*, 662.

Neyrey's argument is less convincing. Methodologically, his attempt is far from obvious because he interprets John in light of the midrashic tradition which appeared later than the Gospel. It is unclear whether John belongs to the same midrashic trajectory. According to Neyrey, the theme of deathlessness is central to the midrashic understanding of Psalm 82, but he never really develops his theory of why John omitted the theme in 10.34-36. He simply explains that John omitted it. The deathlessness, which is decisive for the midrashic understanding, is missing in John 10.34-36. This fact leads us to doubt the possibility that John belongs to the midrashic tradition. I suspect that John did not insert the deathlessness in 10.34-36 since he thought it was not the prerequisite to becoming "gods." The prerequisite was, for John, having the word of God(10.35).

Neyrey posits that in the midrashic tradition God called Israel 'god.' Thus, in Neyrey, the Jewish charge that Jesus, a man makes himself equal to God is erroneous because God makes him "Son of God."[30] However, contrary to Neyrey's interpretation, John does not think that the Jewish charge that Jesus declares himself equal to God is erroneous, since the Johannine Jesus declares himself equal to God: "I and the Father are one"(10.30); "He who has seen me has seen the Father"(14.9). The sentence of the Jewish charge includes "a man"(*anthrōpos*). John disputes against the Jewish notion that Jesus is merely a man and that he has no divinity in his human flesh, and not against the charge that he makes himself equal to God.

In Neyrey, because God gave Israel the word of Torah at Sinai to which the nation became obedient, Israel was called "god."[31] It is not certain whether John keeps the supposed situation of Psalm 82 in his mind when he presents John 10.

29. *Ibid.*, 663.
30. *Ibid.*, 662.
31. *Ibid.*, 648f; C. K. Barrett takes a similar position. *John*, p.384.

Granting it to be true, John's emphasis is changed. John gives the designation "gods" to those to whom the word of God, not the Torah, came. Here John's expression of double meaning[32] is disclosed. Of course Torah was the word of God, but in John the word is another name for Jesus as the prologue of John attests.[33] In other words, John defines those who accepted Jesus as "gods." There is a great gulf between the definition of those who received Torah as "gods" and the definition of those who received the word of God(Jesus) as "gods."[34]

The community members' self-definition as gods is presented in their claim for reciprocal inclusiveness between Jesus or/and God and them. One of the characteristics of Jesus prayer in chapter 17 is the reciprocal inclusiveness between Jesus + God and the believers + other believers(17.20-22,26). This did not appear in the previous chapters. In this sense E. R. Wendland's following assertion[35] is far from obvious.

> There are no dramatic peaks or thoughts and nothing really new here[17] as far as content is concerned, just a basic review of what Jesus had been telling his disciples during his

---

32. On this, see E. Richard, "Expressions of Double Meaning and Their Function in the Gospel of John," *NTS* 31(1985): 96-112.

33. F. F. Segovia regards John 20.30-21.25 as the final farewell of Jesus. He notes that "... this scene, the fourth and final resurrection appearance of Jesus, is said to be particularly concerned with the lasting significance of the figure of Jesus as the Word of God." "The Final Farewell of Jesus: A Reading of John 20:30-21:25," *Semeia* 53(1991): 167-190, esp. 185-187, quoted from 167.

34. W. G. Phillips does not grasp the self-definition of the Johannine community members as "gods" behind 10.34-36. "An Apologetic Study of John 10:34-36," *Bib Sacra* 146(1989): 405-419.

35. E. R. Wendland, "Rhetoric of the Word. An Interactional Discourse Analysis of the Lord's Prayer of John 17 and Its Communicative Implications," *Neotestamentica* 26(1, 1992): 59-88.

entire ministry.[36]

In addition to the reciprocal inclusiveness in 17.20-22,26, Jesus' prayer that God "sanctify them in the truth"(17.17) is also new. Moreover, the notion that Jesus sanctifies himself did not appear in the previous chapters. The idea that Jesus wants the chosen to behold his glory before the foundation of the world is also very new. In this regard, J. N. Suggit's argument that Jesus' prayer in chapter 17 corresponds to the liturgical setting of chapter 13[37] also misses the peculiar color of chapter 17.

Jesus is included in those whom God gave him "out of the world"(17.6a). They were God's(17.6b), and they are still God's(17.9). At the same time they are included in Jesus(15.6,7). John presents three major reciprocal inclusivenesses between Jesus and God, between Jesus and the believers, and between Jesus + God and the believers + other believers. Among them the last one appears nowhere else other than chapter 17. As Jesus and God are in the believers of the community and the other believers "through their words," so they are in Jesus and God expressed by "we"(17.20,21,26). The other believers through other's words, not through "their words," cannot be the beneficiaries of Jesus' prayer.

John 17.11, 20-23 assert the importance of unity between the believers. J. Painter reads the situation between the lines of these verses as follows.

> While the primary reference is to the unity of the believers with God through the revelation in Jesus there is obviously intended in the prayer a consequent unity of the believers in relation to each other. The threat to that unity might well

---

36. *Ibid.*, 78.

37. J. N. Suggit, "John 13-17 Viewed Through Liturgical Spectacles," *Neotestamentica* 26(1, 1992): 47-58.

have emerged in the situation of 'second hand' believers, 17.20ff. It is in this section that the great stress falls on unity and we can suppose that it was this development which brought about the threat of disunity. The 'second hand' believers no longer had a direct link with the Jesus tradition.[38]

Painter's reading of the threat to the unity in 17.20ff. is satisfactory, but his identification of the source of this threat with the 'second hand' believers is less compelling in that the present participle, "those who believe" (*tōn pisteuontōn*) in 17.20 denotes the believers' activity through their word is performed in the present. The expression "through their word" reflects the community's claim that those who believe in Jesus through other believers' word cannot be united to the Johannine community as the divine community.

As God has given Jesus glory, so Jesus has given the same glory to the Johannine community(17.22). As Jesus was executed, the grain of wheat fell onto the earth(12.24), so the community members must prepare to be executed with him. J. A. du Rand interprets John's Gospel in light of discipleship.[39] He posits that

> Johannine discipleship also contributes to a new model of ecclesiology. Discipleship is the self-definition and meaningful function of a community of believers. Discipleship also implies commitment to the community. It constitutes the purpose of the believing community. The community gives the infrastructure to those who believe in Jesus to live as his disciples, to practise fraternal love and to devote themselves to obeying his 'new' command(13:34).[40]

Rand's argument is persuasive except for the phrase "to live

---

38. John Painter, "The Farewell Discourses and the History of Johannine Christianity," *NTS* 27(1981): 525-543, quoted from 541.

39. J. A. du Rand, "Perspectives on Johannine Discipleship according to the Farewell Discourses," *Neotestamentica* 25(2, 1991): 311-325.

40. *Ibid.*, 322.

as his disciples," for John distinguishes between the positive aspects of Jesus' disciples and the negative aspects of them. John exhorts the believers to follow the positive side of the disciples and to disregard their negative side.

Johannes Beutler's exegesis on the death of the grain of wheat in terms of discipleship is very convincing. According to him,

> a final message for the readers of John 12.20-50 is the invitation to follow Jesus until death in fearless confession of faith.... There are reasons to presume that the death which the disciple has to face is not just of spiritual nature or natural death after a long time. It may well be *violent death due to persecution*. This results from 12.42f, the last section, where the theme of "glory"(*doxa*) is resumed in John 12.20-50.[41]

In this sense John agrees with Mark who disagrees with Paul. Paul dehistoricizes the execution of Jesus. He even rejects the significance of the concrete event. For him "flesh and blood cannot inherit the kingdom of God"(I Cor. 15.50). John differs from Mark in his world view, but he concurs with Mark as far as his notice on the significance of flesh is concerned.

John does not assert that Jesus is glorified only after his death. Jesus said, "Now is the Son of man is glorified"(13.31). As Jesus was glorified before his death, so the community members are glorified even before their possible martyrdom. They have already received the glory from Jesus(17.22).

John articulates that Jesus had flesh and his execution was the execution of his flesh. "Blood and water" came from his side after his execution(19.34). As Jesus was executed in terms of the world's maltreatment of his flesh, so the community members must prepare to be executed in terms of the world's extermination of their fleshes. If this is true, why

---

41. J. Beutler, "Greeks Come to See Jesus(John 12,20f)," *Biblica* 71(3, 1990): 333-347, quoted from 346-347. Italics mine.

does John often seem to undermine the flesh(3.6) and the earthly things(3.12). The reason is to be illuminated in light of his method to counterreact against the persecution of the world. John wants to make his community members prepare to follow Jesus until execution which destroys their fleshes. He admonishes the members not to be afraid of the world's persecution which implies the extermination of the flesh. According to John's strategy, the flesh that the world tries to destroy is trivial: "That which is born of the flesh is flesh" (3.6). Through this device John exhorts his community members not to adhere to the flesh when their fleshes are maltreated by the world. Thus, the comforting words of the Johannine Jesus are given to them: "In the world you have tribulation; but be of good cheer, I have overcome the world" (16.33). John often represses the flesh, not because he did not recognize its significance, but because he wants to encourage his community members when their fleshes are exposed to the persecution of the world. He makes the members downgrade the significance of their fleshes and give up their fleshes without hesitation in order to keep their belief in Jesus when the critical hour comes. John encourages the members to prepare the fleshly martyrdom. This is the motif of why John introduces the analogy of a grain of wheat falling onto the earth and dying(12.24a).

The fleshly martyrdom of the community members, however, is transformed into the glory for eternal life as a death of a grain bears much fruit(12.24b). As Jesus goes to the cross by his own decision and he lays down his own life of his own accord(10.18), the community members are encouraged to lay down their own lives of their own accord. John gives the members the social world in which their execution is understood as their glorification, and not their humiliation, as the story of Jesus' passion and resurrection attests. Jesus in John, unlike Jesus in Mark, who utters a cry of despair, shows his confidence through his pronouncement,

"It is finished"(19.30). Therefore, the community members are exhorted to have the same confidence in the critical hour in prospect of their full glorification in heaven.

Jesus' promise of the eternal life does not necessarily imply that the believers never die physically. P. S. Minear distinguishes between the physical death and the death in sin.

> The death from which believers were promised immunity was the death in sin on the part of Adam and his heirs, the wrath and condemnation of God as pictured in Genesis 3(not the death of Gen. 5:5). Those who live "in Christ" will never suffer *that* death. The death that followers of Christ would die was another thing entirely.[42]

Minear's argument is clear-cut and persuasive. The physical death is inescapable for believers, as Minear's argument insinuates. The Johannine believers expect to experience the violent death due to persecution of the world. For them, the natural death could not be transformed into the glory for eternal life. In John the violent death would lead to resurrection and the eternal life. In John's implication, the grain of wheat falls onto the earth, and "must" die in order to bear much fruit. As Jesus as the Son of God was executed, and then was restored to his former glory of his equality to God, so the Johannine community members as children of God will be executed, and then will be restored to their former heavenly status as gods. M. W. G. Stibbe argues that, the elusiveness of

> the Johannine Jesus may reflect the strategies of concealment employed by the Johannine community. The secret movements of John's Jesus may reflect the secrecy enforced upon

---

42. P. S. Minear, "The Promise of Life in the Gospel of John," *TT* 49(1, 1993): 485-499, quoted from 492.

Johannine Christians by the Jewish persecution.[43]

His position on the secrecy in John is convincing, but he does not disclose the content of the secret of the Johannine community. I suspect that the community's secret is that its members had heavenly status as "gods" before they were born on earth and will recover it sooner or later. The prerequisite of the members' full glory is their ascension to heaven after their execution.

In this sense William C. Grese's definition of the Gospel of John as "a manual for a heavenly journey" is impressive and convincing.[44] According to Grese,

> for the evangelist the vision of God, eternal life, the revelation of heavenly secrets – the kind of benefits that others expected to gain via heavenly journeys – are to be found in John.... Taking a tradition that understood baptism as a rebirth that granted entrance into heaven by transforming the one baptized from existence in the flesh to existence in the spirit, he interpreted baptism as a rebirth that would make it possible for the one baptized to see the revelation of God that is available in the life and death of God.[45]

If Grese had answered the question of why John reworked and interpreted the tradition in this fashion, he would secure a more compelling ground. The reason why John emphasizes on the heavenly journey is due to the persecution of the world. The more the persecution is intensified, the more the community members' emphasis on the heavenly journey is deepened.

As long as they live in the social world which points to the

---

43. M. W. G. Stibbe, "The Elusive Christ: A New Reading of the Fourth Gospel," 35.

44. W. C. Grese, "'Unless One is Born Again': The Use of A Heavenly Journey in John 3," *JBL* 107(4, 1988): 677–693.

45. *Ibid.*, 692–693.

heavenly journey as the best mode of spiritual life, their sense of persecution and rejection by the world is transformed in prospect of coming restoration of their heavenly status as gods. The glory in John is a decisive device for his community to survive the vehement persecution of the world. The community members are circulating the secret of their status as gods in the enigmatic language within the community.

Mark L. Appold distinguishes between the idea of the mystery religions and the idea of Gnosticism, although he admits that both have points of convergence in terms of reciprocity and oneness between the divine and the humans.[46]

> In the mystery religions the point at issue is man's transformation or metamorphosis from the terrestrial to the divine by means of external actions, visions, or ecstatic experience. In Gnosis, on the other hand, it is a matter of the realization of divinity which one had always possessed. Here man needs to be awakened out of the stupor of sleep, hear the call of the revealer, and be directed back to the point of his real origin which is the basis of his oneness with the divine world.... In the mystery religions redemption was a process of becoming what one previously was not... whereas in Gnosis man became what he originally was.... In both cases the goal was identification with God.[47]

I suspect that the idea of the Gospel of John is closer to Gnosticism than the mystery religions if we accept Appold's classification, as far as its realization of the reciprocal residence is concerned, although John differs from Gnosticism in the sense of his emphasis on the flesh. In John the believers of the community seek to restore their heavenly

---

46. M. L. Appold, *The Oneness Motif in the Fourth Gospel. Motif Analysis and Exegetical Probe into the Theology of John*(Tübingen: J. C. B. Mohr, 1976), pp.166–174.

47. *Ibid.*, p.167; footnote 3.

origins as the status of gods, not to metamorphose in order to become the divine.

The restoration of the community members' glory is dependent on the peoples' recognition on their divine status as gods. A purpose of John's Gospel is to make the people recognize the community as the divine community. John identifies those people with his community members themselves and with those who believe in Jesus through their word, since it is impossible that all the people on earth recognize the community members as gods. As the world has not known Jesus and his origin(17.25), it also does not know the origin of the community members. The believers are not of the world, as Jesus was not of the world(17.14). The reason why the world hates the believers is that the world does not recognize them as gods.

Thus, the mutual recognition of the believers on their own status as gods is presupposed and stressed. If the believers do not recognize each other as gods, nobody recognizes them as such. This is one of the reasons why John emphasizes the mutual love between the believers: "This is my commandment, that you love one another as I have loved you" (15.12). This mutual love constitutes "a new commandment" (13.34). The mutual love between the believers is a prominent mark for separation of the believers as Jesus' followers from other humans(13.35). Consequently, the community's desire for the restoration of the glory is achieved within itself apart from the recognition of the world. In the community, the members begin the restoration of their former status as gods based on the reciprocal recognition between themselves. They perceive themselves as coexisting gods on the earth. The full restoration of the community's glory, however, is completed by their ascension to heaven.

CONCLUSION

CONCLUSION

This work begins with the reassessment of the so-called standard hypotheses on the origin of the Johannine high christology postulated by R. E. Brown and J. L. Martyn, since the glory in John is predominantly related to the high christology. Although Brown's range of interpretation is broader than Martyn's, both scholars proposed that the social context for the writing of the Gospel was the community's experience of expulsion from the Jewish synagogue. Consequently, both scholars posited that the community began to hold high christology only after the expulsion. The present study argues that the originating group of the Johannine community held high christology even before the expulsion. The high, pre-existence christology does not reflect the social experience of expulsion. Rather, it reflects the community members' conviction that they have heavenly origin. After believing in Jesus, they began to reckon retrospectively that they had been in heaven before they were born on earth.

Contrary to both scholars, the believers held not only the low christology but the high christology as well before the formation of the community. The low christology, which presupposes the flesh of Jesus, legitimates the community's earthly life with limitation of the flesh. The high christology, which retrospects and prospects the glory of Jesus' heavenly status, reflects the community's consciousness of its former and future glory in heaven. The initiation of the community is dependent on these twofold christologies and not on the expulsion from the synagogue. The expulsion did not originate the high christology. Rather it did "reinforce" the high christology to a certain degree.

This research is done from a meso sociological perspective which reconciliates between the micro approach and the macro approach. Meso perspective considers the author(s) of John's Gospel as both the constructor(s) and the constructed of the community. In this position John is regarded as the creative theologian whose theology constrains his community, and at the same time he is the community spokesman whose statements are constrained by the community's proclivity. The role and autonomy of John is neither minimized nor maximazed. They are kept in meso level.

John portrays Jesus as "one who descended from heaven," "one who came down from above" and "one who was sent by God." The meaning of these expressions is that he forfeits his glory of equality to God. John's Gospel begins with the axiom that Jesus is the son of Joseph(humanity) and the Son of God / God(divinity). John has seen both the divinity in Jesus' humanity and the humanity in his divinity. Jesus who has both aspects of humanity and divinity is subordinated to God who has divinity without humanity. God is spirit(3.24). God in heaven has no flesh. In this sense, Jesus the Son of God with the flesh on earth is less than God(13.16).

The divinity of Jesus as the Son of God is retained in his flesh, yet the flesh is not constituted with divinity. The flesh itself is never regarded to be divine in John's Gospel(3.6). Thus, the glory that Jesus reveals through his works on earth is not the same glory that he had with God before the world was made(17.5). The complete restoration of Jesus' former glory is achieved when he rids himself of his humanity and ascends to heaven. Jesus remains unglorified to the fullest, even shortly after his resurrection, since he has "not yet ascended to the Father"(20.17), and still has flesh such as "hands" and "sides"(21.27). One of the reasons why Jesus is less than God(14.28) is that the achievement of Jesus' recovery of his former divine glory is dependent on God's will and His permission.

The Johannine Jesus begins to move toward the former glory through various works. By the use of the term "work"

Jesus consociates his activity with the works of the Father in the past(5.17). In the various works Jesus is portrayed as taking the role of God. Through many disputes against the Jews, the Johannine Jesus claims that he had the glory which includes his equality to God. Jesus' activities on earth in the Gospel of John are to be illuminated in light of his struggle for recovery of the heavenly glory forfeited at the descension.

John presents Jesus as both the Son of God and God. In heaven, Jesus is God, coequal with the Father and fully glorified. On earth, Jesus is the Son of God who has forfeited his equality to the Father. In John, Jesus' full glory as God and his limited glory as the Son of God is distinguished. Although Jesus loses his heavenly status as God, he retains his divinity in the fleshy life as the Son of God(1.14; 2.11). To the evangelist Jesus loses only his glory as God, but to Jesus' opponents he is nothing but the son of Joseph who can be neither the Son of God nor God. Namely, if we paraphrase the idea of the opponents in the evangelist's thought, Jesus loses both his glory as God and his glory as the Son of God.

Since the glory is an interdependent term between the recognizer and the recognized, the glory of Jesus is partly restored when the people recognize him as God's Son sent by Him. John confines the recognizers as those whom the Father gave Jesus out of the world(17.6) because it is impossible that all the people on earth recognize Jesus as God's Son. Those that the Father gave to Jesus know and believe that he is the Son of God sent by God(17.8; 3.16). The full restoration of the forfeited glory of Jesus, however, is completed when he rids of his flesh and departs the earth for heaven. In the time of the Johannine community, Jesus in heaven is considered by the community members to have been completely restored of his former glory as God.

The same scheme of John's portrayal of Jesus can be applied to the life of the Johannine community in terms of its forfeiture of, its struggle for and its restoration of its glory. The members of the Johannine community define themselves as "those born from(*ek tou*) God"(1.13). This expression insinuates that their original dwelling place was in heaven. As Jesus forfeited his divine glory when he came from heaven, the community believers began to reckon that they also forfeited their divine glory when they came from heaven. Although they retain the heavenly origin in their present consciousness, they admit that they were born of flesh and live with flesh on earth like their own contemporaries. The community members on earth are also introduced as "the children of God"(1.12). They are less than Jesus since their status of the children of God is dependent on Jesus. If they do not "receive" him and do not "believe in his name," they cannot become "the children of God."

The community members' works on earth are seen as their struggle for recovery of the glory they forfeited. They are promised to do "greater works than these"(14.12). The expression, "the one who believes"(*ho pisteuon*) as the subjects to perform "greater works" denotes not the apostolic disciples, but the members of the Johannine community. John insinuates that the works of the past disciples through the earthly Jesus is less than the works of the present community members through the heavenly Jesus. This verse, thus, minimizes the significance of the activity of the apostolic Jewish Christians whose present authority is dependent on the past apostles.

The content of "greater works" is neither "the gathering of many converts into the church"(C. K. Barrett), nor "the gathering together of God's scattered children"(R. Schnackenburg), since these are the similar activities that Jesus did, not the "greater works." As the past Jesus did the works to reveal his divinity, so the present community members do the works to reveal his divinity. The community members, however, perform the "greater works" which reveal not merely Jesus' divinity but their own divinities as well.

The Johannine community members conflict with the apostolic Jewish Christians. The apostolic Jewish Christians exercise their own authority from Peter who they claim had a special relationship with the historical Jesus. John reminds them of the past Peter, their ideal leader who did not even know what Jesus was doing(13.8-9). By undermining the foundation of the apostolic Jewish Christians by his critical view of Peter's past activity, John, ostracized by the apostolic Jewish Christianity in the past, reacts to cripple their efforts while validating his own community's presence. Peter is less than the Beloved Disciple in John. All works of Peter are dependent on the Beloved Disciple's witness and report(21.24).

Not only Peter but the other disciples are severely criticized by the Johannine Jesus for their distinction between their belief in God and their belief in Jesus. Jesus has spent "so long" a time not only with Philip but with the disciples, but the latter fails to recognize the former. The present authority of the apostolic Jewish Christians is dependent on the lengthy period of fellowship the past disciples enjoyed with Jesus. John questions the period itself. Despite their lengthy period of fellowship with Jesus, the disciples did not recognize who Jesus really was. John weakens the foundation on which the authority of the apostolic Jewish Christians is dependent. The glory of the Johannine community is partly acquired when its understanding of Jesus is accepted, while the apostolic Jewish Christians understanding is rejected.

As Jesus came forth "from God"(*ek to theou*; 8.42), so the community members came "from God"(*ek theou*; 1.13). Through the expression "from God," John insinuates that the divine origin of Jesus concurs with the divine origin of the Johannine community. Although the community members forfeited their glory as "gods" in heaven when they were born on earth, they retain their glory as the children of God in their consciousness. The community members regard themselves as those who retain the divinity in their humanity. They claim that their community is the divine community since they are children of God.

In the eyes of the evangelist the community members forfeited only their status as "gods," since they retain their status as children of God. In the eyes of the opponents, however, they are neither "gods" nor "children of God." They are nothing but ordinary human beings. If we paraphrase the idea of opponents in the evangelist's style, the community members forfeited not only their glory as "gods" but their glory as children of God. Thus, the restoration of their glory is initiated when the people who initially rejected their claim recognize that they are children of God who were born from God(1.12–13).

The Johannine community members as children of God claim not only to have divine features in themselves but to be "gods." John gives the designation "gods" to those to whom the word of God came(10.34–35). In John the word is another name for Jesus. In other words, John defines those who accepted Jesus as gods. The community members' self-definition as gods is presented in their claim for reciprocal inclusiveness between Jesus or/and God and them. The restoration of the community members' glory as gods is dependent on the peoples' recognition, since the glory is interrelational term between the recognizer and the recognized. John identifies the recognizers with his community members themselves, since it is impossible for all the people on earth to recognize the community members as gods. The mutual recognition of the community members on their status as gods is presupposed and stressed, since the world not only hates but persecutes them.

The Johannine community members do not try to become what they were not previously. Rather, they seek to restore what they were originally. In other words, they seek not to metamorphose in order to become divine, but to regain their former divinity. In fact, within the community the members have restored their former status as gods based on the reciprocal recognition between themselves. They perceive themselves as coexisting gods in the social world of their own community.

Their social world was formulated by the severe maltreatment by the world. They are facing the impending martyrdom. They thought that the martyrdom was inevitable. As Jesus lays down his own life of his own accord(10.18), the community members are encouraged to lay down their own lives of their own accord. The yearning for sharing in Jesus' glory is associated to the inevitability of sharing in his death. The fleshly martyrdom of the members, however, is transformed into the glory for eternal life as the death of a grain bears much fruit(12.24b). As Jesus was glorified before his death(13.31), so the community members are glorified even before their possible martyrdom.

John emphasizes the flesh on one hand(1.14) while he denounces it on the other hand(3.6). According to John's perspective, the former presupposes the human aspect of Jesus and legitimates human life of the Johannine community, while the latter praises Jesus' fleshly martyrdom and encourages the possible fleshly martyrdom of the Johannine community. In John the flesh that the world tries to destroy is trivial: "that which is born of the flesh is flesh(3.6)." Through this device John exhorts his community members not to adhere to the flesh when their fleshes are maltreated by the world. John makes the members disregard their fleshes and give them up without hesitation in order to keep their belief in Jesus when the critical hour comes.

John provides his community members the peculiar symbolic world in which their frustration and fearfulness caused by the persecution of the world are transformed. John downgrades the meaning of the members' fleshes which will be destroyed sooner or later because of the maltreatment by the world: "It is the spirit that gives life, the flesh is of no avail; the words that I have spoken to you are spirit and life"(6.63). Furthermore, "God is spirit"(4.24). The community members are not only children of God but gods in their own consciousness. As Jesus came from the Father, and have come into the world, and was returning to the Father(16.28), so the community members understand their life that they came from God, and have come into the world, and are returning to heaven. As the full restoration of Jesus' glory is completed when he ascends to the former place, so the full restoration of the community members is completed when they ascend to the original place. This social world legitimates and encourages the possible martyrdom of the Johannine community members who thought they could not escape the persecution of the world. This is the reason why John introduces and emphasizes Jesus' consolation: "In the world you have tribulation, but be courageous, I have overcome the world"(16.33).

APPENDIX

Sociological Theory for New Testament Interpretation

APPENDIX
Sociological Theory for
New Testament Interpretation

I . Introduction

Sociological theory attempts to explain pattern and reason of human behavior and seeks to secure the "laws" for them. It focuses not on what happens exclusively inside human minds but on what happens "between" people. Sociological theory is constructed with two constituent elements: concepts and statements. Concepts, such as group, community, power, structure, interaction, conflict, norm, and role are produced by definitions which envisage the phenomenon that is implicated by a concept. Concepts are abstractions; namely, they are ideas, not things. Concepts are interrelated. Interrelations among concepts constitute statements. Statements enumerate the manner in which human behaviors denoted by concepts are connected, and provide an interpretation of why the behaviors could be or should be interrelated. Concepts and statements are the building blocks for theories.

There are three basic approaches in sociological theory for generating theoretical statements: macro approach, micro approach, and meso approach. There are many New Testament scholars who employ sociological approach to their works. They claim their works as "sociological." Most of them, however, are incapable of disclosing clearly on which types of sociology their works are dependent. Howard C. Kee, who is one of a few exceptional scholars, declares quite clearly that "in my own historical work, I have sought to employ the insights and methods of sociology of knowledge."[1] Some sociological theories are not easy to reconcile with one another.[2] The purpose of the present study is to examine the three major sociological approaches and their many subcategories, and to explore their significances and limitations for interpreting the New Testament.

II. Macro Sociological Theory

Macro sociologists concentrate on larger groups, even on whole societies. They attempt to explain the fundamental patterns and processes of large-scale social relations. Macro sociology is divided into two large parts: structuralism and functionalism. Whether macro sociologists emphasize "social structure" or/and "social function," they stand in the same line in that they focus on the forest rather than the trees.

A. Structuralism

In using the term "structuralism" in what follows, I have in mind neither the "linguistical structuralism" of Ferdinand de Saussure and Roman Jakobson nor the "idealistic structuralism" of Claude Lévi-Strauss, but the "social structuralism." Social structuralists are concerned with a social structure which includes characteristics of groups, organizations, and even whole societies. The concept of "social structure" is a metaphor for describing organized set of rules relative to social interrelations that sustain over time.[3]

---

1. Howard C. Kee, *Knowing the Truth. A Sociological Approach to New Testament Interpretation* (Minneapolis: Fortress Press, 1989), p.54.

2. For different major perspectives, for example on social problems, see William Kornblum and Joseph Julian, *Social Problems*, 7th ed. (Englewood Cliffs, New Jersey: Prentice Hall, 1992), pp.4-12.

3. On various definitions of the concept of "social structure", see David Rubinstein, "The Concept of Structure in Sociology," in *Sociological Theory in Transition*, ed. Mark L. Wardell and Stephen

Emile Durkheim, commonly regarded as one of the classical founders of social structuralism, has strongly influenced structural analysis in contemporary social theory. His emphasis on "social fact," which is defined as ways of acting or thinking with the peculiar characteristic of exercising on the individual "an external constraint," was to become one of the major concepts in structuralist analysis. He maintains that

> the first and most fundamental rule is: consider social facts as things.[4]

> The determining cause of a social fact should be sought among the social facts preceding it and not among the states of the individual consciousness.[5]

In Durkheim, what determines the social facts is the "structure of society." According to him, the categories by which individuals perceive the world are determined by the structure and pattern of their social relations. In other words, structures of thought reflect social structural arrangements. As a result, he defines religion as "a unified system of beliefs and practices relative to sacred things ... beliefs and practices which unite into one single moral community called a Church ... the idea of religion is inseparable from that of the Church."[6]

In Durkheim, society is personified in the sacred forces of religions, and so the worship of these forces is, in fact, the

---

P. Turner (Winchester, Mass.: Allen & Unwin, Inc., 1986), pp.80–94.

4. E. Durkheim, *The Rules of Sociological Method*, trans. Sarah A. Solovay and John H. Mueller (Glencoe, Ill.: The Free Press, 1950), p.14.

5. *Ibid.*, p.110f.

6. E. Durkheim, *The Elementary Forms of Religious Life*, trans. Joseph Ward Swain (Glencoe, Ill.: The Free Press, 1948), p.47.

worship of society. Rituals devoted to gods are thus an affirmation of the power of society. He concludes that religion is founded not on the psychological phenomenon, but on the social structure, and gods symbolize this exteriority of society.[7]

The reason why Durkheim emphasizes vehemently the social structure and its exteriority and coercion is to be sought in his intention to dissociate sociology from psychology.[8] Durkheim himself discloses this intention.

> In no case can sociology simply borrow from psychology any one of its principles in order to apply it, as such, to social facts. Collective thought, in its form as in its matter, must be studied in its entirety, in and for itself, with an understanding of its peculiar nature.[9]

---

7. In contrast, Lévi-Strauss' structuralism concluded that the structure of society is but a surface manifestation of fundamental mental processes. Consequently, he denied the ontological status of institution. For informative criticisms on "structuralism" of F. de Saussure and C. Lévi-Strauss, and "post-structuralism" of M. Foucault, J. Lacan and J. Derrida, see Anthony Giddens, "Structuralism, Post-structuralism and the Production of Culture," in *Social Theory Today*, ed. Anthony Giddens and Jonathan Turner(Cambridge, UK: Polity Press, 1987), pp.194-223. "Structuralism, and Post-structuralism also, are dead traditions of thought. Notwithstanding the promise they held in the fresh bloom of youth, they have ultimately failed to generate the revolution in philosophical understanding and social theory that was once their pledge." *Ibid.*, p.195.

8. George Ritzer perceives clearly this point. "Most of Durkheim's work can be recognized as arguments in favor of the social over the psychological... Durkheim stood out only by the explicitness of his attack on psychological reductionism, and by the cleverness of his attempts at proving the autonomy and priority of social structures." George Ritzer, *Sociological Theory*, 3rd ed. (New York: McGraw-Hill, Inc., 1992), p.376f.

Consequently, the role and autonomy of individuals are minimized in Durkheim's stance. Most of the classical sociologists, like A. Comte, K. Marx, H. Spencer took a similar position as far as their concentration on the macro structure of society and its determining force is concerned.

This position whose emphasis on the macro structure of society has been developed by modern sociologists like Bruce H. Mayhew and Peter M. Blau. Mayhew articulates that "in structural sociology the unit of analysis is always the social network, never the individual."[10] Blau is a representative who, more than any others, elaborated the macro structuralism extensively. Blau's position is well epitomized in his proud announcement, "I am a structural determinist."[11] There are various approaches to the study of social structure. In other words, there are different ways of conceptualizing social structure. Blau's focus is on the "pattern of relations between people in society, particularly those of their social relations that integrate society's diverse groups and strata into a distinct coherent social structure."[12] He is concerned with a narrow view of macrostructure.

> Social structure is conceptualized narrowly as referring to the distributions of a population among different social positions that reflect and affect people's relations with one another. To speak of social structure is to speak of differentiation among people. For social structures, as conceptualized, are rooted in the social distinctions people make in their role relations and

---

9. Emile Durkheim, *Emile Durkheim. Selections from His Work*, ed. George Simpson(New York: Thomas Y. Crowell Company, 1963), p.29.

10. Bruce H. Mayhew, "Structuralism versus Individualism: Part I, Shadowboxing in the Dark," *SF* 59(2,1980): 335-375, esp. 349.

11. Peter M. Blau, *Inequality and Heterogeneity: A Primitive Theory of Social Structure* (New York: The Free Press, 1977), p.x.

12. Peter M. Blau, "Elements of Sociological Theorizing," *HJSR* 7(Fall-Winter, 1979-80): 112.

social associations.[13)]

Blau's macrostructural study examines not the networks of all interpersonal relations between individuals, but the patterns of social relations among different social positions employed by many individuals. He defines social position in macrostructural perspective as "common or similar social attributes of people, such as their religion or socioeconomic status."[14)] The social relation between positions of many persons are delineated as the "variable likelihood" or "rate of association" of persons of one position with those of another. A problem in this scheme is in explaining the multiple positions that people occupy. Blau's strategy for controlling this complexity

> is to analyze how the extent to which various types of positions are correlated influences social relations, after having first examined how differences in positions of a single type influence them.[15)]

Blau delineates the structures of societies and communities by two basic types of parameters: "nominal parameter" and "graduated parameter." The former, such as sex, religion, race, and place of residence divides people into different subgroups with distinct boundaries and without rank order. The latter, such as income, wealth, education, and power differentiates people with hierarchical status rank order and without drawing boundaries between strata. All macrostructures, thus, reveal various degrees of differentiation in terms of nominal and graduated parameters. In Blau's scheme, the two forms of differentiation are "heterogeneity" and "inequality." Heterogeneity

---

13. Peter M. Blau, "A Macrosociological Theory of Social Structure," *AJS* 83(1977): 28.

14. *Ibid.*, 29.

15. *Ibid.*, 30.

refers to people distribution in terms of a nominal parameter, while inequality refers to people distribution in terms of graduated parameter.[16]

Blau produces many major theorems.[17] Some of them are listed here. 1. In the relation between any two groups, the rate of intergroup associations of the smaller group exceeds that of the larger. 2. The probability of extensive intergroup relations decreases with increasing group size. 3. The more a majority discriminates in social interrelation against a minority, the smaller is the difference between the majority's lower and the minority's higher rate of intergroup associations. 4. In a pyramidal structure, the rate of social associations of a higher with a lower stratum exceeds the rate of the lower with the higher stratum. 5. Reductions in inequality diminish the impact of status on social associations. 6. Increasing heterogeneity promotes intergroup relations. 7. Intersecting parameters promote intergroup relations. 8. If society's heterogeneity results mostly from heterogeneity within rather than differences among communities, it promotes intergroup and intercommunity relations. 9. If society's inequality results mostly from inequality within rather than differences among communities, it promotes social associations both among different strata in the same community and the same strata in the different communities.

From Blau's detailed theoretical schemes New Testament students could get some significant insights by which to interprete the patterns of the social relations between the primitive Christianity and its contemporary Judaism. Heterogeneity and inequality are the two useful concepts for explaining the characteristics of the intercommunity relations not only between Jewish communities and Christian communities,

---

16. *Ibid.*, 31.
17. *Ibid.*, 35–52, esp.52. Some of selected theorems are paraphrased at a minor level.

but among Christian communities as well. These concepts are effective especially in analyzing both Jewish claims for their racial and religious homogeneity over the Christians and some Christian claims for their hierarchical superiority over other remaining Christians inside and outside the Christian community. Some of Blau's theorems are also useful in exploring the patterns of social associations which are to be strengthened or are to be weakened in a community.

Despite his major contribution to structuralism, Blau's theory is to be criticized, in that social interaction is conceptualized as a rate rather than a process. Jonathan H. Turner indicates this point clearly.

> ... roles are relegated to their effects on parameters; values, beliefs, norms, and other idea systems are eliminated or viewed as relevant only to the extent that they help people define parameters; and the social-psychological properties of the universe, such as self-conceptions and other cognitions of humans, are simply eliminated. Moreover, the theory cannot tell us why a given set of parameters exists in the first place; instead, we are told about their consequences.[18]

In fact, a "desk" exists whether people define it or not. In contrast, "structure" does not exist unless people define it. This phenomenon reveals a certain relationship between structure and humans. Blau's theory, however, disregards this relationship. Rather, his emphasis is on the external parameters which are the determining frameworks for human behaviors. Blau excludes many critical dynamics of the social world to achieve an importance of structural analysis in social theory.

B. Functionalism

---

18. Jonathan H. Turner, *The Structure of Sociological Theory*, 5th ed.(Belmont, California: Wadsworth Publishing Company, 1991), p.581.

Classical functionalists view a society as an integrated system of part. They attempt to explain some part of a system by demonstrating its unintended consequences for some other part of the system. These consequences are termed "function."[19] E. Durkheim, who was regarded as one of the classical representatives not only of structuralism, but of functionalism as well, sought to separate the efficient cause which produces a social phenomenon and the function it fulfills. He used the word "function" in preference to "end" or "purpose." A. R. Radcliffe-Brown took a similar position.[20] Durkheim and Radcliffe-Brown viewed the social world as composed of mutually interrelated parts which are in relation to the maintenance of a systemic whole. This perspective inevitably produces the problems of tautologies and illegitimate teleologies which both functionalists "so unsuccessfully tried to avoid."[21] Functionalistic approaches to social phenomena are considered either conservative or radical. It depends on objects and levels of the assumed function.[22]

Current functionalism is divided into three major types: structural functionalism, empirical functionalism, and systems functionalism.

Talcott Parsons, who is a prominent leader of structural functionalism, advocated a position that the social universe consists of systemic features that must be captured by a parallel ordering of abstract concepts. Parsons conceptualized his action theory by four system requisites: "adaptation," "goal

---

19. Rodney Stark, *Sociology*, 4th ed. (Belmont, California: Wadsworth Publishing Company, 1992), cf. p.101f.

20. A. R. Radcliffe-Brown, *Structure and Function in Primitive Society* (Glencoe, Ill.: The Free Press, 1952), esp. pp.31-50.

21. Jonathan H. Turner, *The Structure of Sociological Theory*, p.50.

22. For ideological assessments of functional approaches, see Robert K. Merton, *Social Theory and Social Structure,* enl.ed (New York: The Free Press, 1968), pp.91-100.

attainment," "integration," which refers to coordination of interrelationships among system units, and "latency," which embraces both pattern maintenance and tension management. In Parsons' functional scheme, specific structures meet the four functional requisites, which, in turn, determine the survival capacity of the social system which is subsystem of the general action system. Parsons' action system was constructed with its four constituent subsystems: culture, social structure, personality, and organism. Each of these subsystems is regarded as fulfilling one of four system requisites of adaptation, goal attainment, integration, and latency.[23] For example, the cultural system is considered to have primary consequences for managing the requisite of latency, while the system of personality has the primary consequences for resolving the requisite of goal attainment.

Parsons' scheme of four system requisites presupposes that if these requisites are not resolved, the system's survival is threatened. But the fundamental question of how one determines "what constitutes the survival and nonsurvival of a system"[24] is not answered by Parsons. Without documenting the determinative items, his theory become tautologous. Despite his elaborate theories,[25] Parsons' functionalism is less useful in establishing sociological theory.

Robert K. Merton, who is a distinguished theorist of empirical

---

23. Talcott Parsons, "An Outline of the Social System," in *Theories of Society*, ed. T. Parsons, E. Shils, K. D. Naegele and J. R. Pitts (New York: The Free Press, 1961), pp.30-38.

24. Jonathan H. Turner, *The Structure of Sociological Theory*, p.76.

25. For the task of establishing the nature of Parsons' permanent contribution to sociological thought, with full-scale comparison between Parsons and his classical predecessors, see Jeffrey C. Alexander, *The Modern Reconstruction of Classical Thought: Talcott Parsons*, vol.4 of *Theoretical Logic in Sociology* (Berkeley: University of California Press, 1983), esp. pp. 73-169.

functionalism, examines three questionable postulates in classical functional analysis: (1) functional unity of society, (2) universal functionalism, (3) indispensability.[26] In regard to the first postulate, Merton, unlike Parsons, emphasizes not on the unity of total systems, but on how the various patterns of social organization within the total system are sustained and altered, both by the requisites of the total system and by interaction among sociocultural items.

> The theoretic framework of functional analysis must expressly require that there be *specification* of the *units* for which a given social or cultural item is functional. It must expressly allow for a given item having diverse consequences, functional and dysfunctional, for individuals, for subgroups, and for the more inclusive social structure and culture. [27]

In regard to the second postulate, unlike Radcliffe–Brown, Merton contemplates the analysis of diverse positive or negative functions of sociocultural items. In respect to the last postulate, Merton stresses that the functional requisites must be established empirically for specific systems. He also posits that alternative structures, rather than only certain structure, can exist to fulfill the same requisites in both similar and diverse systems.

> In contrast to this implied concept of indispensable cultural forms... there is, then, the concept of *functional alternatives,* or *functional equivalents,* or *functional substitutes.*[28]

In his functional strategy, Merton proposes that the analysis of the requisites must be fulfilled by a particular item only after

---

26. Robert K. Merton, *Social Theory and Social Structure,* pp. 79–91.

27. *Ibid.,* p.84.

28. *Ibid.,* p.88.

a description of the structural context in which the item survives. With this pre-description, both the manifest or latent function of an item, and the net balance of positive or negative functions of an item will be established.[29] In sum, Merton stresses empirical functionalism in which each system's diverse needs must be empirically established in all their particulars.

Despite his struggle to avoid the pitfall of tautology, Merton also falls into it in that he posits that if an item persists in an existing system, then it is latently functional for some group. Moreover, in his analysis of political machines, for example, Merton begins not with the phenomenon, but the assumption that they exist to fulfill a function.[30] This is a sort of illegitimate teleology against which he warns. His functionalism is descriptive rather than analytical for the social phenomena, and eventually, it is not proper to establish a theoretical protocol.

Niklas Luhmann, who is an outstanding systems functionalist along with others like Neil J. Smelser and Paul Colomy, has prepared a new way which he calls neofunctionalism.[31] Luhmann's approach is "neo" in the sense that he downgrades functional requisite, which is considered as one of the distinctive notions of previous functionalism. He suggests a "general systems" approach, which presupposes the basic distinction between system and environment.

> General system theory and cybernetics supplanted the classical conceptual model of a whole made out of parts and relations

---

29. *Ibid.*, pp.104-136.

30. Jonathan H. Turner, *The Structure of Sociological Theory*, p.91.

31. For neofunctionalistic approaches, see Jeffrey C. Alexander, ed., *Neofunctionalism* (Newbury Park, CA: Sage, 1985); Paul Colomy, ed., *Neofunctionalist Sociology: Contemporary Statements*(London: Edward Elgar, 1990).

between parts with a model emphasizing the difference between systems and environments. This new paradigm made it possible to relate both the structures (including forms of differentiation) and processes of systems to the environment.[32]

Luhmann proposes three distinct shapes of social systems: interaction systems, organization systems, and societal systems. Interaction systems emerge when individuals are co-present and perceive one another. This embraces "the perception of mutual perception." Individual co-presence is the "selection principle as well as the boundary-formation principle governing interaction systems."[33] The organization systems integrate the actions of individuals with respect to conditions. Organizations are interpolated between the individual interaction systems and the societal systems. Organizations represent a fully distinct development. They coordinate "new principles of boundary-formation and self-selection and can be reduced neither to interaction nor to society."[34] Societal systems are defined as the "all-embracing social system." Society is the "comprehensive system of all reciprocally accessible communicative actions." Society is not merely the sum of all personal interactions. Rather, it is a "system of a higher order."[35] These three types of social systems are mixed together in a very simple society. But, as societies become larger and more complex, these systems become clearly differentiated from and irreducible to one another.

Luhmann explains the complexity of the environment in terms of time. Time is one of the most significant dimensions of the environment. Time is defined as "the social interpretation

---

32. Niklas Luhmann, *The Differentiation of Society* (New York: Columbia University Press, 1982), p.229.

33. *Ibid.*, p.71.

34. *Ibid.*, p.75.

35. *Ibid.*, p.73.

of reality with respect to the difference between past and future."[36] Time, which embodies complex configurations of acts, always presents a system with complexity. Thus, a social system must develop mechanisms for reducing the complexity of time. In Luhmann's scheme, the basic functional requisite is the need to reduce the complexity of the environment in relation to a system of interconnected actions. This point leads us to a critical assessment of Luhmann's functionalism. Luhmann's argument is also teleological: system requisites produce the structures to meet these requisites. In this sense, Luhmann's functionalism is similar to other functionalism, namely, it is not properly "neo" functionalism.

I suspect that all functionalistic approaches including system theory are less useful for interpreting the New Testament, since they have serious theoretical deficiencies respectively. We have separately assessed structuralism and functionalism. Both macro sociological theories, however, take a similar stance in that they strongly emphasize the pre-eminence of the social whole over its individual parts, as Anthony Giddens indicates that

> functionalism and structuralism have some notable similarities, in spite of the otherwise marked contrasts that exist between them. Both tend to express a naturalistic standpoint, and both are inclined toward objectivism.[37]

Macro sociology focuses on the structures, while micro sociology on the actions of individuals. Micro theory revolves around face-to-face interactions among individuals. Stressing the roles and autonomy of individuals, micro theorists attack the macro theorists whose emphasis is on the constraining forces which control its people. The argument that all macro

---

36. *Ibid.*, p.274.

37. Anthony Giddens, *The Constitution of Society. Outline of the Theory of Structuration* (Cambridge: Polity Press, 1984), p.1.

structure is merely aggregated from micro experiences has been proposed by micro theorists to whom we now turn.

III. Micro Sociological Theory

Micro sociology focuses on the role and capacity of the individual within his or her "immediate" social surroundings. Unlike macro sociologists who ask how social structures affect the actions of individuals, micro sociologists ask how individuals create social structures which include the institutions of a society, such as legal and political systems. Micro theorists in the social sciences are interested in "choice" as the most basic aspect of human action. Micro sociologists are always being criticized by macro sociologists that individuals or small groups are usually parts of larger structures, and the characteristics of the actions of the individuals or the laws of the smaller groups are determined in part by the characteristics of the larger. In their response to this criticism, micro sociologists declare not merely that all human groups and institutions consist of the "actions" of individuals in relation to each other, but that sociology is to be concerned with face-to-face interactions among individuals.

Micro sociological theory is divided into two types: exchange behaviorism and symbolic interactionism. The former focuses on the common form of interaction, emphasizing ways in which people reward one another, while the latter on the capacity of humans to create and use symbols as they interact. Both types of micro theory, however, are to be considered to take a similar position in that they concentrate not on the forest, but on the trees.

A. Exchange Behaviorism

Exchange behaviorists who are skeptical of any form of structural and functional theorizing, emphasize on psychological principles as the axioms of social theory. George C. Homans, a representative of this position, maintains that the general principles of all social sciences come from the laws of behavioral psychology. Homans is strongly influenced by B. F. Skinner in the sense that he borrows directly from Skinner's reformulations of behaviorist principles.

Homans argues that actions of the individuals could be explained in terms of the frequency with which the actions were rewarded and punished. Reward and punishment are two basic key concepts for Homans' exchange propositions.[38] Some of Homans' propositions are listed here. 1. Success Proposition: The more often a particular action of a person is rewarded, the more likely the person is to perform that action. 2. Stimulus Proposition: The more a situation approximates one in which a person's action has been rewarded in the past, the more likely the person is to perform the action now. 3. Value Proposition: The more valuable to a person is the result of his action, the more likely a person is to perform the action.

In addition to these propositions, Homans delineates "deprivation-satiation" and "frustration-aggression" propositions in relation to the value factor. The former proposition indicates the condition which qualifies the first three propositions listed above. The more often in the recent past a person's action has received a particular reward, the value of the reward will decrease, and therefore, by the value proposition, the frequency with which he performs the action is likely to go down.[39] The latter proposition, which introduces a form of action in terms of expectation and rate of its realization, determines both the former proposition and

---

38. George C. Homans, *Social Behavior: Its Elementary Form* (New York: Harcourt Brace Javanovich, 1974), pp.11-68.

39. George C. Homans, "Behaviourism and After," in *Social Theory Today*, ed. Anthony Giddens and Jonathan Turner (Cambridge, UK: Polity Press, 1987), p.62.

the first three propositions. If a person's action does not receive the reward he/she expected or receives the punishment he/she did not expect, the person will exhibit anger and aggressive behavior. The aggression is addressed to whatever has produced the frustration. The results of such behavior become more valuable to that person.[40]

Homans' exchange behaviorism shows how patterns of a group are established, maintained, altered, and broken down by the elementary processes of exchange. The relevance of Homans' theory for the study of the New Testament is clear, at least, in a certain subject. There are many themes of motives of reward and punishment in the New Testament. How and why do the writers of the New Testament stress reward and punishment? Both the words, "reward"(*misthos*)[41] and "punishment" (*krima*)[42] appear 28 times respectively in the New Testament. This statistical number will enormously increase if the other words related to them are counted.

The authors of the New Testament seem to perceive that people are motivated by expectations of reward and cost as they interact with one another. The contents of reward consist both of tangible items such as "houses and brothers and sisters and mothers and children and lands"(Mk.10.30), and intangible items such as "kingdom of heaven" (passim), "eternal life"(passim), "comfort"(Mt.5.4), "power to become children of God"(Jn.1.12), "justification"(Gal.2.16; Rom.3.28), and "salvation"(passim). In contrast, the contents of punishment consist both of visible items, such as excommunications(Mt.18. 17; Gal.5.12), and of invisible items such as "being cut down

---

40. *Ibid.*, p.63.

41. Mt.5.12,46; 6.1,2,5,16; 10.41,42; 20.8; Mk.9.41; Lk.6.23,35;10.7; Jn.4.36; Acts1.18; Rom.4.4; I Cor.3.8,14; 9.7,18; I Tim.5.18; Jam.5.4; II Pet.2.13,15; II Jn.8; Jude11; Rev.11.18; 22.12.

42. Mt.7.2; 23.13; Mk.12.40; Lk.20.47; 23.40; 24.20; Jn.9.39; Acts24.25; Rom.2.2,3; 3.8; 5.16; 11.33; 13.2; I Cor.6.7; 11.29,34; Gal.5.10; I Tim.3.6; 5.12; Heb.6.2; Jam.3.1; I Pet.4.17; II Pet.2.3; Jude4; Rev.17.1; 18.20; 20.4.

and thrown into the fire"(Mt.7.19; Lk.3.9), "weeping and gnashing teeth"(Mt.8.12; Lk.13.28), and "wrath and fury"(Rom. 2.8). These are only a few selected instances. There are tremendous amounts of ideas in relation to reward and punishment. Homans' propositions of reward and punishment are useful for identifying both the strategies of leading figures for controlling their followers, and the patterns of followers responding to their leaders in the New Testament.

Homans' propositions, however, come from "a fundamental assumption of behavioral psychology: actions taken in the present feed back to affect future action. Behavioral psychology is thus a fundamentally historical science."[43] In Homans, as a result, sociology reduces to psychology. Homans stresses that sociological patterns could be explained in psychological propositions. He declared himself a "psychological reductionist." He is proud of "W. G. Runciman" who "is prepared to admit that sociology is 'dependent' on psychology."[44]

Homans, who is skeptical of the structures "affecting" the behavior of individuals, gives an example that our behavior to stop our cars on a red light at an intersection is the result of psychological principles.[45] His argument, however, is less convincing. Rather, the behavior seems to be the result of sociological principles. We stop our cars, because we are constrained by a red light which is a social structure. Even when we stop automatically without consciousness, it is not a psychological phenomenon, but a sociological one into which the constraint of a red light is repeatedly incorporated.

I suspect that Homans goes too far. If the laws of sociology are reducible to those of psychology, what is the distinctive feature of sociological laws? There are many sociological

---

43. George C. Homans, "Behaviourism and After," p.60.
44. *Ibid.*, p.77.
45. *Ibid.*, p.73.

phenomena which are never transformed into psychological activities. For the social structure, for example, is "more" than the sum of individual parts. Moreover, the assumption of Homans' propositions, which produce "covering laws"[46] of exchange behaviorism, meet a serious criticism: Do people always count and assess costs and rewards in all situations? This basic question is left by Homans unanswered.

B. Symbolic Interactionism

Symbolic interactionists stress the ability of humans to create and employ symbols. They claim that patterns of social organization among humans are created, sustained, or altered by means of the humans' capacity to create symbols and use them in their interactions. The symbolic interactionists' theories are based on the assumption of George Herbert Mead who is regarded as the founder of symbolic interactionism.[47] Mead used two basic terms: the "mind" and the "self." Mind arises "in the social process only when that process as a whole enters into... the experience of any one of the given individuals involved in that process."[48] Mind is defined as human "understanding of symbols." Self arises "in the process of social experience and activity, that is, develops in the given individual as a result of his relations to that process as a whole

---

46. *Ibid.*, p.68f.

47. R. Stark regards both Charles H. Cooley and George Herbert Mead as the co-founders of symbolic interactionism. Stark, *Sociology*, p.74. It is not a proper assessment, because Cooley was more interested in the social organization and the social order as the titles of his books indicated. See Cooley, *Social Organization*(New York: Scribners, 1909); *Human Nature and the Social Order*(New York: Scribners, 1922).

48. George H. Mead, *Mind, Self and Society: From the Standpoint of a Social Behaviorist*, ed. by Charles W. Morris(Chicago: University of Chicago Press, 1934), p.134.

and to other individuals within that process." Self is defined
by human learned skills to understand the responses of others
to his/her conduct. Where a vocal gesture uttered by one
individual leads to a certain response in another, it may be
called a "symbol" of that act; where it arouses in the
individual who makes it the tendency to the same response, it
may be called a "significant symbol."[49] By interpreting the
vocal gestures of others, humans communicate. Humans have
the capacity to assess each other, to anticipate each other's
responses, and to adjust to each other. In Mead, this capacity
to perceive the other's attitudes is referred to as "taking the
role of other." Humans can only know themselves through the
eyes of others.

> ... this beginning of an act of the other in himself enters into
> his experience, he will find himself tending to act toward
> himself as the other acts toward him. In our self-conscious
> experience we understand what he does or says. The
> possibility of this entering into his experience we have found
> in the cortex of the human brain.[50]

Social control depends on "the degree to which the individuals
in society are able to assume the attitudes of the others"[51]
who are interacted with them. Thus, the self is essentially "a
social structure," and it arises "in the process of social
experience."[52] In his comment on Mead, Herbert Blumer
declares that "I wish to stress that Mead saw the self as a

---

49. George H. Mead, "The Genesis of the Self and Social
Control," in *The Sociological Perspective. Introductory Readings*, ed.
McNall(Boston: Little, Brown and Company, 1968), p.141. This article
appeared originally in *IJE* 35(1925): 251–273. It is reprinted in the
present anthology.

50. *Ibid.*, p.140f.

51. *Ibid.*, p.143.

52. George H. Mead, *Mind, Self and Society*, p.140.

process and not as a structure."[53] This declaration, however, comes from Blumer's less careful reading of Mead. In Mead, self is considered not merely as a process, but as "a social structure" in that it can be an object to itself.[54]

Although all of the current symbolic interactionists share the basic assumption of Mead, they have selectively adopted his ideas. Herbert Blumer and Manford Kuhn are the representatives of the contemporary symbolic interactionists. Blumer represents the so-called "Chicago School," while Kuhn the so-called "Iowa School."[55] Blumer and Kuhn show their agreements and disagreements over several areas.[56] Both Blumer and Kuhn stress that the interaction is dependent on the people's capacity to interpret symbols. However, there is divergence over the nature of interaction. Blumer emphasizes interaction as a constant process of role taking with others and groups, while Kuhn emphasizes the dependent nature of interaction upon the process of role taking. In Blumer, self is an important object that enters into people's definitions, while in Kuhn, people's "core self is the most important object and constraint on interaction."[57] Both scholars agree that social

---

53. Herbert Blumer, "Sociological Implications of Thought of George Herbert Mead," in *Sociological Theory*, ed. W. L. Wallace (Chicago: Aldine Publishing Company, 1969), p.235.

54. George H. Mead, *Mind, Self and Society*, p.140.

55. J. H. Turner claims that these labels are inappropriate. For the reasons he gives, see his *The Structure of Sociological Theory*, p.391f.

56. For the excellent and well-digested comparison between the two scholars, see *ibid.*, pp.392-409. For Blumer, see *Symbolic Interactionism: Perspective and Method* (Englewood Cliffs, NJ: Prentice-Hall, 1969); For Kuhn, see "Major Trends in Symbolic Interaction Theory in the Past Twenty-Five Years," *SQ* 5(Winter, 1964): 61-84. The following comparisons are drawn predominantly from J. H. Turner in an epitomized form.

57. J. H. Turner, *The Structure of Sociological Theory*, p.396f.

structure is created and changed by processes of symbolic interaction. However, in Blumer, social structure is dependent upon constant readjustments as actors' definitions and behaviors change. In Kuhn, although symbolic interactions create and change structures, once these structure are created they operate to constrain interaction.[58]

Blumer and Kuhn take a similar position that sociological methods must concentrate on the processes by which people define situations. However, Blumer emphasizes that sociological methods must seek to explain the humans' mental world, while Kuhn emphasizes that they must seek to explain humans' symbolic processes. In regards to sociological theory, Blumer stresses that the "sensitizing concepts," which provide clues and suggestions about where to look for certain classes of phenomena, and which offer a general sense of what is relevant to approach flexibly a shifting empirical world, are only possible in sociology. Thus, deductive theory is not possible in sociology. In constrast, Kuhn stresses that sociological theory must develop defined concepts with empirical measures. It can be deductive with a limited number of general propositions which include empirical generalizations on different aspects of symbolic interactionism.[59] I suspect that Kuhn is more convincing than Blumer in all areas of disagreement, for Kuhn presupposes a strong link between interaction and social structure, especially including the constraining character of the latter on the former. But even Kuhn is incapable of suggesting the concrete items for that link.

The implications of symbolic interactionism for New Testament study are illuminating. Many stories about Jesus and his followers or opponents recorded in the Gospels can be understood in terms of symbolic interactions between them.

---

58. *Ibid.*, p.397f.
59. *Ibid.*, pp.398–405.

Jesus had a great capacity to create the significant symbols and use them in various interactions with his contemporaries. By interpreting the vocal gestures of others, especially those of the Jewish leaders, such as Pharisees and Sadducces on one hand, and those of his sympathizers, such as his disciples and his immediate followers on the other hand, Jesus anticipated their actions and gave restriction on them in order to adjust them on his behalf. Insights from symbolic interactionism lead the New Testament scholars to perceive the prime social reality of situational negotiations, and its significance for their study.

Despite their contribution to sociological theory in the sense of introducing the · importance of micro aspects, however, symbolic interactionists do not elaborate on what types of structures are established and altered by what types of face-to-face interaction in what types of contexts. Their strategy will be more persuasive if their efforts concentrate on exploring concepts and propositions linking the interaction process to the social structure as its result.

IV. Meso Sociological Theory

Some recent sociologists propose a reconciliation between macro approach and micro approach. They endeavor to remove the gap between the two approaches and to explore the possible links between subject and object, action and structure, and individual and society. These attempts can be termed the "meso" approach. Meso theorists concentrate on the relationship between the forest and the trees.

Peter Berger is one of the pioneers in favor of the macro-micro linkage. With the insights from social phenomenology of Alfred Schutz,[60] who was influenced by Max

---

60. Alfred Schutz and Thomas Luckmann, *The Structures of Life-World* (Evanston: Northwestern University Press, 1973), esp.

Weber and Edmund Husserl, Berger, along with Thomas Luckmann, analyzes the society in terms of both "objective reality" and "subjective reality."[61]   Berger perceives the reality of everyday life.

> The world of everyday life is not only taken for granted as reality by the ordinary members of society in the subjectively meaningful conduct of their lives. It is a world that originates in their thoughts and actions.[62]

He proceeds to the argument that "the objectivity of the institutional world, however massive it may appear to the individual, is a humanly produced, constructed objectivity."[63] G. Ritzer unfairly criticized this aspect of Berger's thought. It is necessary to examine Ritzer's model which is one-sided and is not recommended, in order to eliminate a similar inappropriate understanding of Berger. Ritzer's summary of *The Social Construction of Reality* is the following.

> Berger and Luckmann argued that reality itself is not something that is there for researchers to investigate, but something that is produced by people in everyday life. Hence the major subject for sociologists to study is not social institutions and macrostructures, since these do not exist independently of human reality-constructors. It is, rather, the principles of social phenomenology. Sociologists should examine the structure of social experience itself.[64]

This is only a part of Berger's scheme, for Berger stresses

Chapters II, and IV.

61. Peter Berger and Thomas Luckmann, *The Social Construction of Reality. A Treatise in the Sociology of Knowledge* (New York: Doubleday & Company, 1967), esp. Chapters II, and III.

62. *Ibid.*, p.19f.

63. *Ibid.*, p.60.

64. George Ritzer, *Sociological Theory*, p.383.

humans' capacity to produce a world that they "experience as something other than a human product."[65] The product, then, constrains back on the producer. The relationship between humans(the producer) and the social world(their product) are dialectical for Berger.

> *Society is a human product. Society is an objective reality. Man is a social product.* It may also already be evident that an analysis of the social world that leaves out any one of these three moments will be distortive.[66]

These three moments are termed "externalization," "objectivation," and "internalization" respectively. In Berger, two essential features of constructing a social world are institutionalization and legitimation. This socially constructed world is internalized into consciousness in the process of socialization.[67]

Erving Goffman is another leading theorist of sociology of everyday life who attempts to integrate the two realms. Goffman's issue centers around the analysis of micro social processes which include face-to-face interaction among individuals. He never establishes, however, his work as an attack on the macro-sociological perspective. Unlike many who advocate micro-analysis, Goffman does not claim that the interaction order is all that is real.

> ... to speak of the relatively autonomous forms of life in the interaction order... is not to put forward these forms as somehow prior, fundamental, or constitutive of the shape of

---

65. P. Berger and T. Luckmann, *The Social Construction of Reality*, p.61.

66. *Ibid.*, p.61. Italics author's.

67. On the significance of Berger's sociology of knowledge for the New Testament interpretation, see Howard C. Kee, *Knowing the Truth*, pp.50–55.

macroscopic phenomena. To do so is akin to the self-centering game of playwrights, clinical psychologist, ... all of whom fit their stories out so that forces within individual characters constitute and govern the action.[68]

Goffman argues that macro phenomena are not to be explained by micro-level analysis. Rather, macro phenomena constrain the general forms of interaction. Thus, it is possible to turn Durkheimian theory to the level of everyday life interactions. The dynamics of the interaction itself, however, preclude a one-to-one relation to these structural phenomena. The notion that even the particular forms of interaction are constrained by macrostructure is crude in that it disregards the autonomy of the interaction order.

> From the perspective of the physical and biological sciences, human social life is only a small irregular scab on the face of nature, not particularly amenable to deep systematic analysis. And so it is. But it's ours ... Only in modern times have university students been systematically trained to examine all levels of social life meticulously.[69]

Goffman presents his own sociological self as the practitioner picking over the details of everyday social life.

Goffman's perception that the "interaction order" is a distinct realm that cannot explain more macrostructural phenomena and that can only be loosely combined with them, and his perception that the constraining power of macro realm on the everyday life interaction is restricted only to its general forms represent a moderated position on the micro/macro question. Goffman's concentration on important concepts as the titles of his books, *The Presentation of Self in Everyday Life*,[70] *Interaction Rituals*,[71] and *Forms of Talk*,[72]

---

68. Erving Goffman, "The Interaction Order," *ASR* 48(1983): 9.
69. *Ibid.*, 17.

has influenced the recent scholars such as Anthony Giddens and Randall Collins,[73] whose emphasis is on micro/macro integration. Goffman has allowed the macro theorists to recognize the importance of interactionist theory, and the micro theorists to draw legitimation of their works upon him, though both theorists are cautious of, and critical of his theory.

The works on micro-macro linkage are attempted either in a larger scale, or in a smaller scale. Strictly speaking, however, most works on the integrations of micro and macro realms are not accomplished at the level of perfect balance between the two sides. Rather, the efforts on the integration are attempted by emphasizing more of the micro realm or the macro realm.

Jeffrey C. Alexander, who once expressed an interest in the relationships between collective order and individual order, and between instrumental action and normative action, turns to grant strong priority to collective order and normative action. Alexander criticizes all theories that have their origins at the micro level. He maintains that any micro perspective is to be abandoned because it terminates with "randomness and complete unpredictability" rather than order. In Alexander, the theoretical framework of sociology is to be deduced only from a macro perspective.[74] He declared his choice for collective-

---

70. (New York: Doubleday & Company, Inc., 1959).

71. (New York: Doubleday & Company, Inc., 1967).

72. (Philadelphia: University of Pennsylvania Press, 1981).

73. For Goffman's influence on Giddens, see Giddens, "Erving Goffman as a Systematic Social Theorist," in *Social Theory and Modern Sociology* (Cambridge, UK: Polity Press, 1987), pp.109-139; His influence on Collins, see Collins, "Micromethods as a Basis for Macrosociology," *UL* 12(2,1983): 184-202. Collins' major concepts such as "interaction ritual" and "deference and demeanor" are drawn from Goffman.

74. Jeffrey C. Alexander, ed., *Neofunctionalism*, p.27f.

normative theories. This is why he shows the adherence to classical macro theorists.

> I suggest that a 'neo-functionalist' tradition based on a reconstructed Parsons and his classical foundations remains possible. ... Durkheim's ideas on structure yet play a significant role.[75]

As a result, Alexander's contribution is negligible as far as the linkage between macro and micro realms is concerned.

In contrast to Alexander, George Ritzer expresses strong interest in the "dialectical relationship" among all levels.[76] According to Ritzer, macro social realms and micro social realms are to be classified as either objective or subjective, respectively. Along this classification, he proposes four levels: 1. Macro-objective which includes society, law bureaucracy, architecture technology, and language; 2. Macro-subjective which includes culture, norms, and values; 3. Micro-objective which includes patterns of behavior, action, and interaction; 4. Micro-subjective which includes the various facets of the social construction of reality. In Ritzer's scheme, each of these four major levels of social analysis is important itself, "but of utmost importance is the dialectical relationship among and between them."[77]

There are two prominent attempts to integrate the micro-macro realms: structuration theory of Anthony Giddens, and interaction ritual chains of Randall Collins. The former is concerned with constructing a "meso theory" between the two theories in terms of theoretical synthesis, while the latter with establishing a "meso level" between the two ranges in terms

---

75. Jeffrey C. Alexander, "The Centrality of the Classics," in *Social Theory Today*, ed. Anthony Giddens and Jonathan Turner (Cambridge, UK: Polity Press, 1987), p.45.

76. George Ritzer, *Sociological Theory*, p.546.

77. *Ibid.*, p.544.

of units of middle range.

A. Structuration Theory

Indicating the limits of structuralism, functionalism, and interactionism, Giddens offers the structuration theory. Structuration theory emphasizes on the relationship between agency and structure. Agency and structure involve each other. The structuration is proposed as means to reject dualisms of micro versus macro realm and action versus structure in sociological theory, and to characterize the dichotomies as "duality." Structure, which is constituted by rules and resources, is what gives form and shape to social life, but it is not itself that form and shape. Structure as memory traces is out of time and space.[78] In contrast, the social systems in which structure is recursively implicated, are understood as reproduced activities across time and space. Systems have structures or at least 'structural properties'; they are not themselves structures. Agents in interaction use the rules and resources of social structure, and so doing, they reproduce these rules and resources of structure. Thus individual activities and social structure are closely interrelated.

> The constitution of agents and structures are not two independently given sets of phenomena, a dualism, but represent a duality. According to the notion of the duality of structure, the structural properties of social systems are both medium and outcome of the practices they recursively organize. Structure is not 'external' to individuals... it is in a certain sense more 'internal' than exterior to their activities in Durkheimian's sense.[79]

---

78. Anthony Giddens, *The Constitution of Society. Outline of the Theory of Structuration*, p.25.
79. *Ibid.*, p.25.

Giddens admits the constraining character of structure on action, but he posits that structure is always "both constraining and enabling."[80] Structures often enable agents to do something. Agents can be coerced by structures, but such a coercion is not inevitable.

For Giddens, "agency" implies the events that an agent achieves · rather than "intentions," or "purposes." In other words, agency is what an agent actually does in a situation. Humans "reflexively monitor" their own behavior and that of others. The reflexive monitoring, which is the purposive of intentional character of human behavior, is influenced by two levels of consciousness: "discursive consciousness" and "practical consciousness." The former is what actors can express about social conditions, including especially the conditions of their own action, and rationalize them discursively, while the latter is what actors believe about social conditions, including especially the conditions of their own action, but cannot express discursively.[81]

In discursive consciousness, human agents are not only able to monitor their activities and those of others, but are also able to 'monitor that monitoring.'[82] The concept of practical consciousness is also "fundamental to structuration theory. It is that characteristic of human agent or subject to which structuralism has been particularly blind... there are barriers ... between discursive consciousness and the unconscious."[83] In Giddens, unconscious motivation is a significant feature of human conduct. There are many pressures to act in certain ways, which an agent does not perceive. The level of motivation is unconscious, and also, for Giddens, the most divorced from action itself.[84] Repetitive activities have regularized

---

80. *Ibid.*, p.25.
81. *Ibid.*, pp.5-8.
82. *Ibid.*, p.29.
83. *Ibid.*, p.7.

consequences, unintended by those who are involved in those activities. The unintended consequences are regularly dispersed and maintained by regularized behavior of agents. In Giddens, structure is "actively produced, reproduced, and transformed by the capacities of agents."[85] Thus, structural analysis is reconnected to the processing of interaction.

Giddens has proposed a detailed analysis for agency-structure integration. G. Ritzer's assessment of Giddens is exemplary.

> What is most satisfying about Giddens' approach is the fact that his key concern, structuration, is defined in inherently integrative terms. The constitutions of agents and structures are not independent of one another; the properties of social systems are seen as both medium and outcome of the practices of actors, and those system properties recursively organize the practices of actors.[86]

Although there is a major deficiency in his theory in the sense that it consists of a series of definitions which are not precisely interwoven together, Giddens' works, which represent a seminal breakthrough in the integrating efforts between macro and micro domains, are prominent and promising. The implications of Giddens' view for New Testament study are profound. Giddens' works are effective to postulate both the autonomy and heteronomy of the New Testament writers. Giddens' works make it plausible to assume that they not only control, but are controlled by, their own communities which produced the New Testament.

B. Interaction Ritual Chains

---

84. Ian Craib, *Anthony Giddens*, (New York: Routledge, 1992), p.37.

85. J. H. Turner, *The Structure of Sociological Theory*, p.536.

86. G. Ritzer, *Sociological Theory*, p.574.

Randall Collins' concern revolves around how to reconcile between the micro and macro levels. He attempts to reduce the gap between the two levels by positioning intermediate units: organizations and stratification systems. Collins postulates the co-presence of at least two individuals as the basic micro unit of interaction. He begins to analyze the basic unit in terms of the exchange of resources and rituals. A ritual contains not only the elements of common focus of attention, mutual awareness, and common emotional mood, but symbolization of these three elements in some way.

In an encounter, each individual comes with three resources acquired in previous chain of encounters: 1. emotional energy, 2. conversational or cultural capital, and 3. a social reputation.[87] Each encounter combines resources of different individuals. In a given interaction ritual, a particular individual attains ritual membership, while other(s) fails to attain it, and one dominates over other(s), while other(s) is subordinated. This phenomenon depends on how individuals combine the three resources.

> The interaction is marketlike, in the sense that each individual tacitly compares the degree of conversational, emotional, and (perhaps) reputational payoffs he or she is getting from interacting with this person, compared to the other interactions he or she feels are available. Hence some interactions come off, others do not; and some come off in a symmetrical form(interaction among equals), others in asymmetrical form (interaction among dominants and subordinates).[88]

One of the asymmetrical form of interaction is deference and demeanor. Collins defines "deference" as the process of manipulating talks/gestures to show respect to others, or to

---

87. Randall Collins, "Micromethods as a Basis for Macrosociology," 191f.

88. *Ibid.*, 191.

elicit respect from others, and "demeanor" as the actual manipulation of talks/gestures. Deference and demeanor, which tend to become ritualized, can be sought "in terms of the structure of the power and solidarity found in any society."[89] A presupposition of deference and demeanor is inequality in resources, particularly wealth and power among varying numbers of people.

Some of Collins' numerous principles[90] on deference and demeanor are the following: 1. The more unequal the power resources and the higher the surveillance, the more often acts of petty ritual deference and demeanor are demanded. 2. The more unequal the power resources and the lower the diversity of communications, the more extensive the formality of conversational manners. 3. The greater the degree of inequality, and the less the degree of mobility, the more visible and predictable are deference and demeanor rituals and talks.

Interaction rituals and exchanges occur in groups which are ingrained in organizational system such as bureaucracies and associations, and stratificational system such as classes and power groupings. Interaction rituals sustain both systems which in turn, constitute a society. The larger-scale macrostructures, such as political empires, are constructed with conquest of different societies. Thus, as these ritualized chain of exchanges include larger number of people and are outspread in space and time, macrostructure are generated and maintained.

Collins stresses that all macrophenomena can be translated "into combination of micro events," and "microtranslation strategy reveals the empirical realities of social structures as repetitive micro-interaction."[91] Collins seeks to dissociate

---

89. Randall Collins, *Conflict Sociology* (New York: Academic Press, 1975), p.171.

90. *Ibid.*, pp.216-219.

himself from macro theories and their concerns with macro level phenomena. It does not mean that he rejects macro reality as a phenomenon. Rather it implies that the macro realm is constructed from repetition of, or chains of ritual interaction. Collins also seeks to distance himself from the extreme micro levels whose concentration on the thought and action of individual is separated from more macro phenomena. By proposing "interaction ritual chains," Collins avoids effectively the extreme microsociology. By analyzing the encounter as the basic unit of interaction, Collins argues that

> the focus of micro-macro connection is not the individual. The individual is really larger than an encounter; what we think of as the individual or the self is to a certain degree a *macro*reality, since he or she is made up of many encounters. In a sense this is very radical, since we reduce the individual to the encounter.[92]

Thus, Collins' so-called "radical microsociology" attempts not to reduce sociology to psychology, but to reduce macro-sociology to microsociology. If it is the encounter of individuals rather than the individuals themselves that produces the foundation for the larger structure, the basic unit is still sociological.[93] Collins recognizes that there are three pure macro variables which are "irreducible macrofactors": space, time, and numbers of individuals involved. Except for these inevitable variables, all macro events can be translated into aggregations of micro events.[94]

---

91. Randall Collins, "On the Microfoundations of Macrosociology," *AJS* 86(1981): 984-1014, esp.985.

92. Randall Collins, "Micromethods as a Basis for Macrosociology," 190.

93. *Ibid.*, 190.

94. Randall Collins, "On the Microfoundations of Macrosociology," 989.

The relevance of Collins' propositions on interaction ritual chains for the New Testament, particularly for the Pauline epistles is clear. Paul's responding actions to the behaviors of his community members can be illuminated in terms of deference and demeanor. The propositions on deference and demeanor also give a fruitful way to look at the dynamics among the community members whose material, symbol, and power resources are basically in inequality.

Collins' work is filled with creative insights which give a useful way to look at the social world in terms of interaction ritual chains. If his effort is devoted to producing explicit formulation of his numerous implicit theoretical propositions on interaction ritual chains, Collins' work will be more provocative and convincing.

V. Conclusion

Micro sociologists accuse macro sociologists of making reality out of concepts such as system and structure. They consider social structure as nothing more than the processes of micro interaction among individuals. In contrast to them, macro sociologists argue that such interaction is constrained by the structures of society. Extreme structuralist, like P. Blau, analyzes structure without reference to the processes behind the structure and to interaction or symbolic resources employed by individuals. Extreme interactionist, like G. C. Homans, who fails to address the theme of structure, seeks to reduce sociology to psychology.

Meso sociologists who recognize these deficiencies of macro and micro theories, seek to integrate between the two. Among micro, macro, and meso approaches, the promising is the meso approach. Meso theoretical efforts to link between micro and macro realms are attempted either by emphasizing on the micro level(R. Collins) and vice versa(J. C. Alexander), or by focusing on the dialectical relationship between them (A. Giddens).

The allusion that meso efforts are more promising than the other two approaches, however, does not mean that sociologists must necessarily reject the macro and micro spheres. There is still a continuing need for extending knowledge of those spheres respectively. Rather, it means that there must be a new way to grasp all the social phenomena which embrace from the minute everyday life interactions to the grand structures of society. In fact, meso direction takes a considerable step beyond the macro or micro way in the sense that it opens a door for the new task.

Meso approach is highly instructive for the New Testament studies since it gives an implicit insight that the writers of the New Testament are not merely projects of each communities by which the document are produced but dynamic projectors of each communities as well. In macro approach, the authors of the New Testament are considered to be predominantly constrained by their own communities; their roles and autonomies are minimized in this stance. In micro approach, the authors are considered to determine the nature and shape of communities; their roles and autonomies are maximized in this stance. In meso approach, however, the writers of the New Testament or the protagonists described in it are regarded to influence, or to be influenced by, their communities. They are both constructors and the constructed of their communites.

Meso sociological theory will be more fruitful if it directs to integrate micro and macro theories by emphasizing on the macro level from a micro-theoretical orientation and vice versa. Current meso sociological attempts are by no means complete. Not only meso but other approaches are in the same situation. Recently(1992), Randall Collins described this point clearly. Sociological "theories are not all worked out; and there are considerable areas of genuine disagreement and much research yet to be done."[95] Sociological interpretations of the New Testament are also not complete. New Testament scholars, who employ one or some of these diverse sociological theories, are demanded to declare explicitly on which sociological theories their works are dependent in order to save the term "sociological" from their vague use of it. Furthermore, it should be a prerequisite for New Testament scholars to examine and to assess the strong or weak points of sociological theories themselves, before they employ them in their works. New Testament scholars are also requested to go one step forward in the exploration of new sociological theories, if they desire to rid of themselves of their dependence on sociologists. Not only the sociologists but New Testament scholars as well, are responsible for constructing the new sociological theories.

---

95. Randall Collins, *Sociological Insight. An Introduction to Non-Obvious Sociology*, 2nd ed.(Oxford: Oxford University Press, 1992), p.viii.

Abbreviations

ABR	Australian Biblical Review
AJS	American Journal of Sociology
ASR	American Sociological Review
BR	Biblical Research
Bib Re	Bible Review
Bib Sacra	Bibliotheca Sacra
CBQ	Catholic Biblical Quarterly
HJSR	Humboldt Journal of Social Relations
IJE	International Journal of Ethics
IrTQ	Irish Theological Quarterly
JAAR	Journal of the American Academy of Religion
JBL	Journal of Biblical Literature
JETS	Journal of the Evangelical Theological Society
JSNT	Journal for the Study of the New Testament
NTS	New Testament Studies
Nov Test	Novum Testamentum
SF	Social Forces
SJT	Scottish Journal of Theology
SQ	Sociological Quarterly
TT	Theology Today
UL	Urban Life
ZNW	Zeitschrift für die Neutestamentliche Wissenschaft
ZTK	Zeitschrift für Theologie und Kirche

Selected Bibliography

Alexander, J. C. *The Modern Reconstruction of Classical Thought: Talcott Parsons, vol.4 of Theoretical Logic in Sociology.* Berkeley: University of California Press, 1983.

_____. "The Centrality of the Classics." In *Social Theory Today*, pp.11-57. Edited by A. Giddens and J. Turner. Cambridge, UK: Polity Press, 1987.

_____. ed. *Neofunctionalism.* Newbury Park, CA: Sage, 1985.

Appold, M. L. *The Oneness Motif in the Fourth Gospel. Motif Analysis and Exegetical Probe into the Theology of John.* Tübingen: J. C. B. Mohr, 1976.

Ashton, J. *Understanding the Fourth Gospel.* Oxford: Clarendon Press, 1991.

_____. "The Transformation of Wisdom. A Study of the Prologue of John's Gospel." *NTS* 32(1986): 161-186.

Bammel, E. "Die Abschiedsrede des Johannesevangeliums und Ihr Jüdischer Hintergrund." *Neotestamentica* 26(1, 1992): 1-12.

Barrett, C. K. *The Gospel According to St John. An Introduction with Commentary and Notes on the Greek Text*, 2nd ed. London: SPCK, 1978.

Bartholomew, G. L. "Feed My Lambs: John 21:15-19 As Oral Gospel." *Semeia* 39(1987): 69-96.

Beasley-Murray, G. R. *John*. Word Biblical Commentary 36. Waco, Texas: Word Books, 1987.

Berger, P. and Luckmann, T. *The Social Construction of Reality. A Treatise in the Sociology of Knowledge*. New York: Doubleday & Company, 1967.

Beutler, J. "Greeks Come to See Jesus(John 12,20f)." *Biblica* 71(3, 1990): 333-347.

Blau, P. M. *Inequality and Heterogeneity: A Primitive Theory of Social Structure*. New York: The Free Press, 1977.

_____."A Macrosociological Theory of Social Structure." *AJS* 83(1977): 26-54.

Brown, R. E. *The Community of the Beloved Disciple*. New York: Paulist Press, 1979.

_____. *The Gospel According to John*, 2vols. New York: Doubleday & Company Inc., 1966, 1970.

Brown, R. E., Donfried, K. P. and Reumann, J. eds. *Peter in the New Testament*. New York: Paulist Press, 1973.

Bultmann, R. *The Gospel of John. A Commentary*. Philadelphia: The Westminster Press, 1971.

Burkett, D. *The Son of the Man in the Gospel of John*. Sheffield, England: Sheffield Academic Press, 1991.

Caird, G. B. "The Glory of God in the Fourth Gospel: An Exercise in Biblical Semantics." *NTS*(1969): 265-277.

Carter, W. "The Prologue and John's Gospel: Function, Symbol and the Definitive Word." *JSNT* 39(1990): 35-58.

Cassidy, R. J. *John's Gospel in New Perspective Christology and the Realities of Roman Power*. Maryknoll, New York: Orbis Books, 1992.

Charlesworth, J. H. "Reinterpreting John. How the Dead Sea Scrolls Have Revolutionized Our Understanding of the Gospel of John." *Bib Rev* 9(1, 1993): 19-25, 54.

Cleary, M. "Raymond Brown's View of the Johannine Controversy: Its Relevance for Christology Today." *IrTQ* 58(4, 1992): 292-304.

Collins, R. *Sociological Insight. An Introduction to Non-Obvious Sociology*. 2nd ed. Oxford: Oxford University Press, 1992.

_____. "On the Microfoundations of Macrosociology." *AJS* 86(1981): 984-1014.

_____. *Conflict Sociology*. New York: Academic Press, 1975.

_____. "Micromethods as a Basis for Macrosociology." *UL* 12(2, 1983): 184-202.

Colomy, P.ed. *Neofunctionalist Sociology: Contemporary Statements*. London: Edward Elgar, 1990.

Cook, W. R. "The 'Glory' Motif in the Johannine Corpus." *JETS* 27(3, 1984): 291-297.

Craib, I. *Anthony Giddens*. New York: Routledge, 1992.

Cullmann, O. *The Johannine Circle*. Philadelphia: The Westminster Press, 1976.

Culpepper, R. A. "The Pivot of John's Prologue." *NTS* 27(1981): 1-31.

Dietzfelbinger, C. "Die Größeren Werke(John 14:12f)." *NTS* 35(1989): 27-47.

Dillow, J. C. "Abiding Is Remaining in Fellowship: Another Look at John 15:1-6." *Bib Sacra* 147(1990): 44-53.

Domeris, W. R. "The Farewell Discourse. An Anthropological Approach." *Neotestamentica* 25(1991): 233-250.

Draper, J. A. "The Sociological Function of the Spirit/Paraclete in the Farewell Discourses in the Fourth Gospel." *Neotestamentica* 26(1, 1992): 13-29.

Droge, A. J. "The Status of Peter in the Fourth Gospel: A Note on John 18:10-11." *JBL* 109(2, 1990): 307-311.

Du Rand, J. A. "Perspectives on Johannine Discipleship According to the Farewell Discourses." *Neotestamentica* 25(2, 1991): 311-325.

_____. "A Story and A Community: Reading the First Farewell Discourse(John 13:31-14:31) From Narratological and Sociological Perspective." *Neotestamentica* 26(1992): 31-45.

Evans, C. A. "On the Prologue of John and the Trimorphic Protennoia." *NTS* 27(1981): 395-401.

Giddens, A. "Structuralism, Post-structuralism and the Production of Culture." In *Social Theory Today*, pp.194–223. Edited by A. Giddens and J. Turner. Cambridge, UK: Polity Press, 1987.

_____. *The Constitution of Society. Outline of the Theory of Structuration*. Cambridge: Polity Press, 1984.

_____. "Erving Goffman as a Systematic Social Theorist." In *Social Theory and Modern Sociology*, pp.109–139. Cambridge, UK: Polity Press, 1987.

Goffman, E. *Forms of Talk*. Philadelphia: University of Pennsylvania Press, 1981.

_____. "The Interaction Order." *ASR* 48(1983): 1–17.

Goulder, M. "Nicodemus." *SJT* 44(2, 1992): 153–168.

Grese, W. C. "'Unless One is Born Again': The Use of A Heavenly Journey in John 3." *JBL* 107(4, 1988): 677–693.

Grigsby, B. "Washing in the Pool of Siloam – A Thematic Anticipation of the Johannine Cross." *Nov Test* 27(3, 1985): 227–235.

Gundry, R. H. "'In my Father's House are many Monai' (John 14.2)." *ZNW* 58(1967): 68–72.

Haenchen, E. *John* II. Philadelphia: Fortress Press, 1984.

Homans, G. C. *Social Behavior: Its Elementary Form*. New York: Harcourt Brace Javanovich, 1974.

_____. "Behaviourism and After." In *Social Theory Today*, pp.58–81. Edited by A. Giddens and J. Turner. Cambridge,

UK: Polity Press, 1987.

Jervell, J. *Jesus in the Gospel of John.* Minneapolis: Augsburg Publishing House, 1984.

Johnston, G. "Ecce   Home! Irony in the Christology of the Fourth Evangelist." In *The Glory of Christ in the New Testament. Studies in Christology,* pp.125-138. Edited by L. D. Hurst and N. T. Wright. Oxford: Clarendon Press, 1987.

Käsemann, E. *The Testament of Jesus. A Study of the Gospel of John in the Light of Chapter 17.* Philadelphia: Fortress Press, 1968.

Kee, H. C. *Community of the New Age. Studies in Mark's Gospel.* Philadelphia: The Westminster Press, 1977.

_____. *Jesus in History. An Approach to the Study of the Gospels.* 2nd ed. New York: Harcourt Brace Jovanovich Inc., 1977.

_____. *Knowing the Truth. A Sociological Approach to New Testament Interpretation.* Minneapolis: Fortress Press, 1989.

_____. "Myth and Miracle: Isis, Wisdom, and the Logos of John." In *Myth, Symbol and Reality,* pp.145-164. Edited by Alan M. Olson. Notre Dame & London: University of Notre Dame Press, 1980.

Kelber, W. H. "In the Beginning were the Words. The Apotheosis and Narrative Displacement of the Logos." *JAAR* 58 (1, 1990): 69-98.

_____. "The Birth of A Beginning: John 1:1-8." *Semeia* 52(1990): 121-144.

Koester, C. R. "The Savior of the World(John 4:42)." *JBL* 109(4, 1990): 665-680.

Kornblum, W. and Julian, J. *Social Problems*. 7th ed. Englewood Cliffs, New Jersey: Prentice Hall, 1992.

Kysar, R. "John's Anti-Jewish Polemic." *Bib Rev* 9(1, 1993): 26-27.

Lieu, J. M. "Blindness in the Johannine Tradition." *NTS* 34(1988): 83-95.

Loader, W. R. G. "The Central Structure of Johannine Christology." *NTS* 30(1984): 188-216.

Luhmann, N. *The Differentiation of Society*. New York: Columbia University Press, 1982.

Malatesta, E. "The Spirit/Paraclete in the Fourth Gospel." *Biblica* 54(1973): 539-550.

Martyn, J. L. *The Gospel of John in Christian History*. New York: Paulist Press, 1979.

Mastin, B. A. "A Neglected Feature of the Christology of the Fourth Gospel." *NTS* 22(1975): 32-51.

Mayhew, B. H. "Structuralism versus Individualism: Part I, Shadowboxing in the Dark." *SF* 59(2, 1980): 335-375.

Maynard, A. H. "The Role of Peter in the Fourth Gospel." *NTS* 30(1984): 532-548.

Mealand, D. L. "The Christology of the Fourth Gospel." *SJT* 31(1978): 449–467.

Meeks, W. A. "Equal to God." In *The Conversation Continues– Studies in Paul and John. In Honor of J. Louis Martyn,* pp.309–321. Edited by Robert T. Fortna and Beverly R. Gaventa. Nashville: Abingdon Press, 1990.

_____. "The Man from Heaven in Johannine Sectarianism." *JBL* 91(1972): 44–72.

Menken, M. J. J. "The Translation of Psalm 41.10 in John 13.18." *JSNT* 40(1990): 61–79.

Miller, E. L. "The Logic of the Logos Hymn: A New View." *NTS* 29(1983): 552–561.

Minear, P. S. *John. The Martyr's Gospel.* New York: The Pilgrim Press, 1984.

_____. "The Promise of Life in the Gospel of John." *TT* 49(1, 1993): 485–499.

Müller, U. B. "Die Parakletenvorstellung in Johannes-evangelium." *ZTK* 71(1974): 31–77.

Newman, C. C. *Paul's Glory – Christology: Tradition and Rhetoric.* Leiden: E. J. Brill, 1992.

Neyrey, J. H. *An Ideology of Revolt. John's Christology in Social-Science Perspective.* Philadelphia: Fortress Press, 1988.

_____. " 'I said: You are gods': Psalm 82:6 and John 10." *JBL* 108(1989): 647–663.

_____. " 'My Lord and My God': The Divinity of Jesus in John's Gospel." In *SBL Seminar Papers*, pp.152-171. Atlanta, Georgia: Scholars Press, 1988.

Nicol, W. *The Sēmeia in the Fourth Gospel*. Leiden: E. J. Brill, 1972.

O'Day, G. R. " 'I Have Overcome the World' (John 16:33) Narrative Time in John 13-17." *Semeia* 53(1991): 153-166.

Painter, J. "Christology and the History of the Johannine Community in the Prologue of the Fourth Gospel." *NTS* 30(1984): 460-474.

_____. "John 9 and the Interpretation of the Fourth Gospel." *JSNT* 28(1986): 31-61.

_____. "Christology and the Fourth Gospel. A Study of the Prologue." *ABR* 31(1983): 45-62.

_____. "The Farewell Discourses and the History of Johannine Christianity." *NTS* 27(1981): 525-543.

Pamment, M. "The Meaning of Doxa in the Fourth Gospel." *ZNW* 74(1973): 12-16.

Philips, W. G. "An Apologetic Study of John 10:34-36." *Bib Sacra* 146(1989): 405-419.

Pryor, J. W. "Jesus and Israel in the Fourth Gospel - John 1:11." *Nov Test* 32(3, 1990): 201-218.

_____. "Of the Virgin Birth or the Birth of Christian? The Text of John 1:13 Once More." *Nov Test* 27

(4, 1985): 296-318.

Reim, G. "Jesus as God in the Fourth Gospel: The Old Testament Background." *NTS* 30(1984): 158-160.

Reinhartz, A. "Jesus as Prophet: Predictive Prolepses in the Fourth Gospel." *JSNT* 36(1989): 3-16.

Richard, E. "Expressions of Double Meaning and Their Function in the Gospel of John." *NTS* 31(1985): 96-112.

Ritzer, G. *Sociological Theory*. 3rd ed. New York: McGraw-Hill Inc., 1992.

Robinson, J. A. T. *Redating the New Testament*. Philadelphia: The Westminster Press, 1976.

Schnackenburg, R. *The Gospel According to St John*. 3vols. New York: The Seabury Press, 1980; The Crossroad Publishing Company, 1982.

Schutz, A. and Luckmann, T. *The Structures of Life-World*. Evanston: Northwestern University Press, 1973.

Segovia, F. F. "The Final Farewell of Jesus: A Reading of John 20:30-21:25." *Semeia* 53(1991): 167-190.

_____. "The Structure, Tendenz and Sitz im Leben of John 13:31-14:31." *JBL* 104(3, 1985): 471-493.

_____. " 'Peace I Leave with You: My Peace I Give to You': Discipleship in the Fourth Gospel." In *Discipleship in the New Testament*, pp.76-102. Edited by F. F. Segovia. Philadelphia: Fortress Press, 1985.

Sloyan, G. *John*. Atlanta: John Knox Press, 1988.

Snyder, G. F. "John 13:16 and the Anti-Petrinism of the Johannine Tradition." *BR* 16(1971): 5-15.

Stark, R. *Sociology*. 4th ed. Belmont, California: Wadsworth Publishing Company, 1992.

Stibbe, M. W. G. "The Elusive Christ: A New Reading of the Fourth Gospel." *JSNT* 44(1991): 19-37.

Suggit, J. N. "John 13-17 Viewed Through Liturgical Spectacles." *Neotestamentica* 26(1, 1992): 47-58.

Thompson, M. M. *The Humanity of Jesus in the Fourth Gospel*. Philadelphia: Fortress Press, 1988.

Tobin, T. H. "The Prologue of John and Hellenistic Speculation." *CBQ* 52(2, 1990): 252-269.

Turner, J. H. *The Structure of Sociological Theory*. 5th ed. Belmont, California: Wadsworth Publishing Company, 1991.

Wallace, D. B. "John 5,2 and the Date of the Fourth Gospel." *Biblica* 71(2, 1990): 177-205.

Wendland, E. R. "Rhetoric of the Word. An Interactional Discourse Analysis of the Lord's Prayer of John 17 and Its Communicative Implications." *Neotestamentica* 26(1, 1992): 59-88.

Woll, D. B. *Johannine Christianity in Conflict: Authority, Rank and Succession in the First Farewell Discourse*. Chico: Scholars Press, 1981.

Wuellner, W. "Putting Life Back into the Lazarus Story and Its Reading: The Narrative Rhetoric of John 11 as the Narration of Faith." *Semeia* 53(1991): 113–132.

Index of Modern Authors